BIG IDEAS
LITTLE PICTURES

EXPLAINING THE WORLD
One Sketch at a Time

JONO HEY

Creator of Sketchplanations

TABLE OF CONTENTS

All the Sketchplanations you'll find inside, organized by topic.

NATURE'S NUANCES
The wonders and subtleties of the natural world.

HEALTH AND HEALING
Self-care and well-being, both personal and public.

THERE'S A WORD FOR THAT
Terms and concepts that help explain our world.

MOTIVATION AND INSPIRATION
Collected wisdom and insight you can apply anytime.

BLIND SPOTS
How our brains, eyes and experiences mislead us.

STARRY-EYED SURPRISES
The sky, space and our place in it.

BUSINESS AND BYTES
Technology and economics in our professional and personal lives.

THINKING ABOUT THINKING
Our minds at work, and how to improve them.

THE BIG PICTURE
Reframing our personal perspectives.

LIFE'S LITTLE MANUALS
Helpful hacks and handy tips to make every day a better one.

A TOOLKIT
FOR LIFE

I'VE ALWAYS BEEN DRAWN TO IDEAS that help me better understand the world.

For me, a healthy stockpile of concepts, mental models and frameworks to draw on is a reliable toolkit for every day. When I face a problem, I can reach into my toolkit and find something to move me forward. Other times, an idea gives me a greater understanding of the world, enriching my everyday life.

For the past decade, through my site and newsletter, Sketchplanations, I've gathered some of the most useful and interesting ideas I've come across—the ones I reach for again and again—and presented them in an easy-to-digest format: the sketch. Drawings make concepts quick to learn and help them stick in your brain—after all, what good is a tool if you can't find it when you need it? This book includes nearly 150 of these sketches.

The ideas in the book loosely belong to one of four categories: our world,

our lives, our cultures and our well-being, with a smattering of popular wisdom for good measure. For me, part of the joy of Sketchplanations has always been the diversity of topics—none of us are one-dimensional, after all—so in that spirit, I've mixed the ideas in the book so you can dip in, start from anywhere and enjoy a surprise at each page turn. Plus, I've connected sketches covering similar topics with handy footnotes. I hope these sketches inspire you in the same way these ideas inspired me.

Sir Arthur Eddington, an English astrophysicist, once told a story about a scientist studying fish by catching them in nets. After checking the haul each time, the scientist concludes there must be a minimum size for fish in the sea, since he never found any smaller than a certain size. But the littlest ones had just slipped through the net, unmeasurable. The instrument you use affects what you see. Or, as American mathematician Richard Hamming puts it, "You get what you measure."

This analogy provides a concrete example of a phenomenon that routinely affects us in subtler ways. What and how we choose to measure affects our conclusions. A website may easily measure sales and bounce rates for its pages, while factors like trust, authority or satisfaction—which may be more significant longer-term metrics—go unmeasured.

As Hamming points out:
> *"There is always a tendency to grab the hard, firm measurement, though it may be quite irrelevant as compared to the soft one, which in the long run may be much more relevant to your goals.* **Accuracy** *of measurement tends to get confused with* **relevance** *of measurement, much more than most people believe."*

SEE ALSO
The Coastline Paradox, *14*
Understanding Reliability and Validity, *192*

Despite our best intentions, accidents happen. The authors of a paper analyzing accidents in large, complex systems—such as power stations or plane crashes—conclude that "no one failure, human or technical, is sufficient to cause an accident. Rather, it involves the unlikely and often unforeseeable conjunction of several contributing factors arising from different levels of the system."

Psychology professor James Reason's Swiss cheese model is a memorable visual metaphor that illustrates how each safeguard may contain a latent flaw, or hole, and that an unfortunate circumstance may result in these holes lining up to potentially disastrous effect. It's also a nice reminder that multiple layers of defense will always be more effective at mitigating risk, but even with our best efforts, there's still potential for something to go wrong.

SEE ALSO
Pour, Don't Dip When Sharing Snacks, *150*
Dracula Sneeze, *196*
Physics Envy, *240*

THE SWISS CHEESE MODEL

FOR UNDERSTANDING ACCIDENTS AND IMPROVING SAFETY

ANY SAFEGUARD HAS INHERENT FLAWS OR "HOLES"

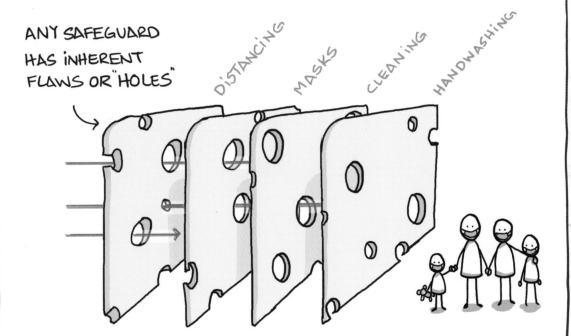

PROBLEMS OCCUR WHEN MULTIPLE "HOLES" LINE UP

It's pretty hard to come to terms with the scale of our solar system. To help process its vast distances, astronomers use astronomical units, where 1 AU is the distance from Earth to the sun. If you see Venus (our closest neighbor at just 0.7 AU from the sun) in the night sky, it looks impossibly far away. But the farther out you go, the more the distances multiply. Earth and Venus are practically on top of each other compared to Uranus and Neptune; the latter is a full 30 times the distance of Earth from the sun.

Now think about the fact that our little solar system is over 250,000 AUs from the nearest star, which is just one of many tucked away in a small corner of the Milky Way, which in turn is only one of many galaxies that make up the known universe. It might be time to sit down.

SOLAR SYSTEM SIZES

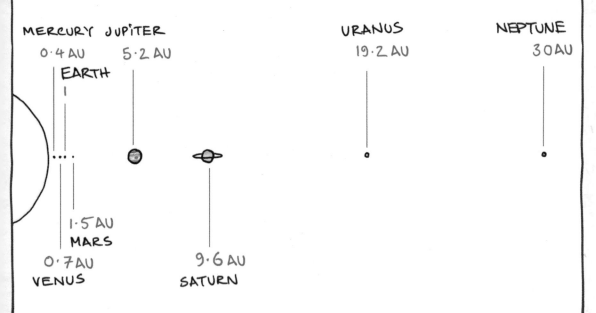

MERCURY   JUPITER
0.4 AU   5.2 AU

EARTH

1.5 AU
MARS

0.7 AU
VENUS

9.6 AU
SATURN

URANUS
19.2 AU

NEPTUNE
30 AU

1 AU ~ 150 million km

Astronomical unit   Average distance from Earth to the Sun

How long is a coastline? The answer isn't as straightforward as you might think. If you were to calculate the coastline of a country by measuring on a globe, you would come out with a vastly different number than if you were to pace around the edge. The closer you look at a coast, the more wiggles and general squiggliness you come across. The smaller your ruler, the longer the coastline gets.

This phenomenon was first spotted in the 1960s by an Englishman named Lewis Fry Richardson when checking his theory that the likelihood of war between countries depends on the length of their shared borders. To his surprise, he found that the quoted lengths of national borders varied significantly. While measuring on maps of different scales, he saw that the smaller the scale of the map, or the smaller the width of the calipers he measured with, the more the length increased.

When looking at coastlines instead of borders, some countries have more jagged coasts, so the length increases at a faster rate with the scale. For instance, Norway's coastline, with its crinkly fjords, increases faster than Britain's, which in turn increases faster than South Africa's. The rate of this increase later became known as the fractal dimension. This phenomenon is present in other things we try to measure: river networks, brains, frequencies, lightning or even stock market trends.

SEE ALSO
Double-Landlocked Countries, *110*
Understanding Reliability and Validity, *192*

THE COASTLINE PARADOX

COASTLINE LENGTH DEPENDS ON HOW YOU MEASURE IT

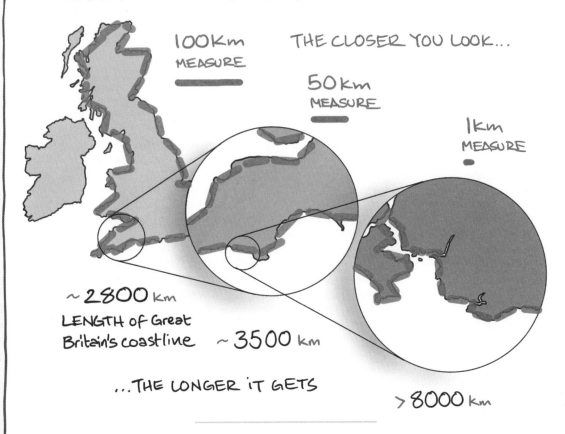

100Km
MEASURE

THE CLOSER YOU LOOK...

50km
MEASURE

1km
MEASURE

~ 2800 km
LENGTH of Great
Britain's coastline   ~ 3500 km

...THE LONGER IT GETS

> 8000 km

THE RATE LENGTH INCREASES . FRACTAL   (its wiggliness)
WITH SCALE IS THE . DIMENSION

Monopoly is the board game people love to hate, responsible for satisfying victories and explosive arguments. These tips, drawn from gaming experts and competitive Monopoly players, can help you up your game.

1. There are many ways to end up in jail, which means people will often start their turns from there after they get out. As a result, the properties after jail are the most frequented.

2. Utilities and railroads are rarely worth the money you put into them, plus you can't build houses on them.

3. Money sitting in your hand isn't working for you. Aim to balance your cash reserves to maximize property investment that earns money for you while leaving just enough for emergencies.

4. The benefit of building three houses is higher than that of fewer houses or adding a fourth. Aim to get all properties to three houses before extending farther.

5. If you make it to the game's end stages, consider a three-turn stay in jail rather than risking landing on others' properties. What this strategy suggests about capitalism is up to reader interpretation.

SEE ALSO
Skip Rocks Like a Pro, *254*

HOW TO WIN AT MONOPOLY
STRATEGIES TO IMPROVE YOUR ODDS

BUY ORANGE + RED
Properties after jail
are landed on more

SKIP UTILITIES + RAILROADS
Only 3% chance to pay back
+ no upgrading

STAY IN JAIL
Late in the
game to
save $

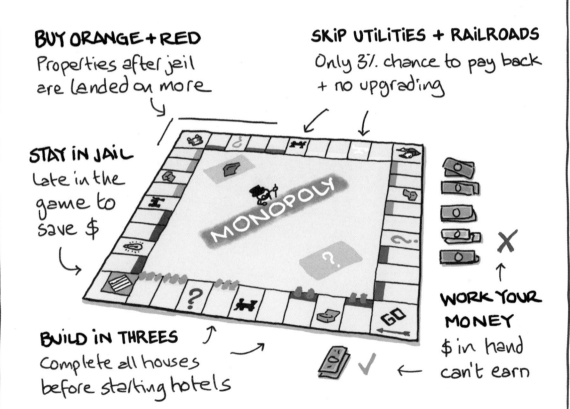

**WORK YOUR
MONEY**
$ in hand
can't earn

BUILD IN THREES
Complete all houses
before starting hotels

While standing in front of a grand view, you may notice that the colors of the objects, hills or mountains in the distance seem less vivid than those nearby. If there's mist, fog, dust or pollution, the effect is more pronounced. That's atmospheric perspective at work, a phenomenon by which distant objects lose their intensity and color as light travels through more air to reach you. On a blue sky day, the objects take on a bluer tone, ultimately blending into the color of the sky in the distance.

SEE ALSO
The Golden Ratio, *128*
One, Two and Three-Point Perspective, *202-207*

ATMOSPHERIC PERSPECTIVE
COLORS AND INTENSITY FADE WITH DISTANCE

Lighter/
Faded

LOW CONTRAST + SATURATION

Closer to the color of the sky

Distance

Intense/
colorful

HIGH CONTRAST + SATURATION

Mist, dust or fog increases the effect

The Doppler effect is the change in frequency of a wave as its source moves relative to the observer.

The most recognizable example of this effect is the change in pitch of the siren on a vehicle as it drives past, but the Doppler effect is also used to estimate blood flow with ultrasound and measure the speed of a passing car or pitcher's fastball. It can even determine the motion of the stars. Doppler shift-based satellite navigation was also the first operational use of the system that eventually led to GPS.

When a siren or similar noise approaches, I try to imagine the crunching up of the sound waves—the vehicle seemingly chasing after its own sound—and the way the waves stretch as it heads past and into the distance. At least it distracts me a little from the unpleasantly loud noise.

SEE ALSO
States of Matter, *96*

THE DOPPLER EFFECT

CHANGE IN PERCEIVED FREQUENCY DUE TO RELATIVE MOTION

STATIC SOURCE

MOVING SOURCE

FREQUENCY SHIFTED LOWER   FREQUENCY SHIFTED HIGHER

Ah, that satisfying, superior, at once gleeful and slightly sinful feeling when the aggressive driver that blazed past you a few miles back is pulled over by the police at the next exit. That feeling is schadenfreude (a nifty German word made up of "schaden" for damage, harm or hurt and "freude" for joy), the act of taking pleasure in others' misfortunes.

I hadn't thought much of it before reading some excerpts from Tiffany Watt Smith's book *Schadenfreude*. She makes a compelling case for the benefits of examining the moments when we feel superior at another's expense as a small window into ourselves. A little twinge of joy when a colleague doesn't get a promotion might reveal your jealousy of their situation or a deep-down resentment of unfairness. If the person who pushed in front of you in line drops their ice cream right after buying it, your secret twinge of joy might be a sense of justice and equity for obeying the rules when they didn't. Schadenfreude can be a little boost to your own self-esteem or a valuable window into your own weaknesses.

SEE ALSO
The Awkwardness Vortex, *246*

SCHADENFREUDE

damage   *joy*

PLEASURE AT SOMEONE ELSE'S MISFORTUNE

"THE REVENGE OF THE IMPOTENT"

— FRIEDRICH NIETZSCHE

It's natural to draw correlations from what we see in front of us. But what we see usually represents a tiny part of everything that happened. Focusing on the evidence we can easily see at the expense of what we can't see is survivorship bias.

When we see a Volkswagen Beetle, first manufactured in 1938, it's tempting to think, "We don't make cars like we used to," happily ignoring all the vintage cars in the scrap heap. Or because Bill Gates dropped out of college to start Microsoft, it might seem like dropping out would be a path to success for others too. But that ignores all the dropouts who didn't create Microsofts and whom we didn't hear about. And from the headlines, it might seem like investment fund managers always make great investment returns, cheerfully neglecting all the fund managers who disappeared without ever making the front pages.

Simply put, we usually only see the winners. The losers tend to disappear from the record.

SEE ALSO
You Get What You Measure, *8*
The Paradox of Choice, *50*

SURVIVORSHIP BIAS

WE OFTEN OVERLOOK THE "SILENT EVIDENCE" OF HISTORY'S LOSERS

When a giant tree falls in a forest where the trees grow tall and straight, like those in the U.S. Pacific Northwest, it creates an opening in the forest canopy that lets in light for new growth. The mighty fallen tree trunks then provide a surface for seedlings to take root, away from the competition of the forest floor. When this happens, the fallen tree becomes an integral part of a new ecosystem.

These fallen trees are known as nurse logs. Sometimes a nurse log is so successful as a nursery for young trees that they will grow along the full length of the fallen trunk. When the nurse log finally decays, it leaves behind a remarkable, straight line of trees.

SEE ALSO
Who Cut Down the Last Tree?, *36*
The Square-Cube Law, *140*

From the combination of the Latin words sol (sun) and sistere (to stand still), the solstice marks the highest or lowest points of the sun's path in the sky each year.

The sun's path through the sky changes each day by a small amount In summer, the sun's arc stops its daily ascent on the longest day of the year. There, it reverses course, beginning its descent to the autumnal equinox—with equal day and night—and eventually to its lowest point at the year's shortest day, the winter solstice. At that point, the sun once again begins its slow climb toward the summer solstice.

SEE ALSO
Seasons, *32*
Equinox, *46*

SOLSTICE

WHEN THE SUN REACHES ITS MOST NORTHERN OR SOUTHERN
ARC IN THE SKY EACH YEAR

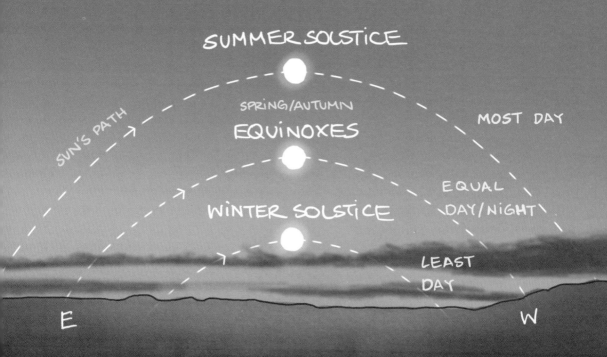

SUMMER SOLSTICE

SPRING/AUTUMN
EQUINOXES

SUN'S PATH

MOST DAY

WINTER SOLSTICE

EQUAL
DAY/NIGHT

LEAST
DAY

E

W

The changing seasons are caused by Earth's tilt. As Earth goes around the sun, the tilt of Earth's axis—23.5 degrees—causes the Northern and Southern Hemispheres to be either tilted toward the sun or away from it at different times of year.

In winter, the Earth's tilt means that the sun's light is spread over a larger area. This makes it weaker and creates a season of colder weather.

In summer, light from the sun hits more directly so it's concentrated on a smaller area, leading to hotter days.

The tilt also means that seasons are reversed in the two hemispheres, so if it's winter in the Northern Hemisphere, it's summer in the Southern Hemisphere and vice versa. The farther from the equator you go, the larger the effect of the seasons. For example, temperatures in Ecuador stay relatively constant throughout the year, while the poles experience extremes of 24-hour daylight or 24-hour night, as well as great freezes and thaws.

SEE ALSO
Autumn Leaves, *90*
Phases of the Moon, *176*

SEASONS

CAUSED BY THE EARTH'S TILT

WINTER

SOLAR ENERGY IS SPREAD OVER A LARGER AREA
MAKING IT WEAKER

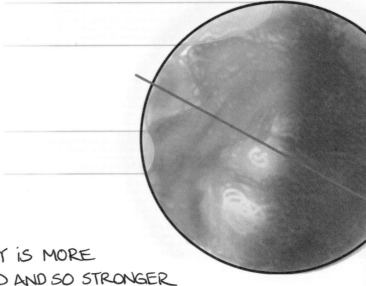

SUMMER

SOLAR ENERGY IS MORE
CONCENTRATED AND SO STRONGER

Animals don't pick the names we use for them, and sometimes the names that stick are downright confusing. Starfish, for example, aren't fish. They are echinoderms, a separate family of sea creatures whose name loosely means "spiny skin" in Greek. For that matter, jellyfish aren't fish either, and of course, seahorses aren't horses.

Its reputation as a killer no doubt influenced the name of the killer whale—more properly known as the orca—yet it's actually the largest of the dolphin family. A dog-like bark earned prairie dogs their name even though they're a type of burrowing ground squirrel. Meriwether Lewis, of Lewis and Clark fame, called it the "barking squirrel."

Red pandas have been placed in several animal families, including one that's unique to them. Guinea pigs aren't swine—they're rodents. Koala bears aren't bears; they're marsupials with a eucalyptus diet that is so lacking in nutrients that they sleep around 20 hours a day. And the poor mountain chicken is actually a huge frog (also known as the giant ditch frog) that tastes like chicken.

SEE ALSO
Animals That Regenerate, *186*
Sacred Animals, *256*

Not a fish

STARFISH

Raccoon? Bear? Kind of its own thing

RED PANDA

Rodent!

GUINEA PIG

bark!

Really a type of squirrel

PRAIRIE DOG

MISLEADING ANIMAL NAMES

?! Big frog

MOUNTAIN CHICKEN

In the dolphin family

KILLER WHALE

Marsupial

KOALA BEAR

If you lived on Easter Island, would you really cut down the last mighty tree knowing the island would be forever barren? It seems either foolhardy or desperate to knowingly destroy the last of a kind, not to mention your last source of timber. So how could it happen?

Jared Diamond, in his book *Collapse* and article "Easter's End," explains how this could happen through a gradual, hardly noticeable decline over many years. Islanders who remembered the great trees that used to provide rafts, canoes and ships were old or had long since died. The trees seen at the end may have been nothing like the forests and towering trunks of tens or hundreds of years before.

As Diamond puts it, "Gradually trees became fewer, smaller, and less important. By the time the last fruit-bearing adult palm tree was cut, palms had long since ceased to be of economic significance. That left only smaller and smaller palm saplings to clear each year, along with other bushes and treelets. No one would have noticed the felling of the last small palm."

SEE ALSO
The Continental Axis Hypothesis, *116*
1.5 Billion Heartbeats, *130*

WHO CUT DOWN THE LAST TREE?

DISASTERS CAN HAPPEN NOT WITH A BANG BUT WITH A WHIMPER

300 YRS AGO   100 YRS AGO   TODAY

"NO ONE WOULD HAVE NOTICED THE FELLING OF THE LAST SMALL PALM."

— JARED DIAMOND ON EASTER ISLAND

You have to drop off two things after school, do your shopping and get back home. Which route should you take? Or let's say you drive a delivery van and have 145 packages to deliver across a big, sprawling city—what's the most efficient route?

It's pretty clear that for situations like the first, with fewer stops, you could figure out the best route by trying out the different combinations until you hit on the shortest. The trouble is, as you keep adding extra stops, it doesn't get just a little bit harder—the difficulty increases exponentially, as does the time it takes to solve the problem.

Figuring out the shortest route to visit all the stops and return back home is known as the traveling salesman problem. While first recognized over 150 years ago, it still holds relevance and interest today, whether for delivering packages, stocking shelves or running errands. There are many approaches to getting good answers quickly using combinations of algorithms and heuristics, and the solutions are a source of competitive advantage for companies that do it well. The value of efficient solutions is clear: UPS calculated the cost of each of their drivers driving one additional mile each day at $30 million!

SEE ALSO
Idempotence, *112*
Decimal vs. Binary, *138*

THE TRAVELING SALESMAN PROBLEM
WHAT'S THE SHORTEST ROUTE TO ALL STOPS AND BACK?

ADDING MORE STOPS TAKES

LONGER AND LONGER AND LONGER TO FIGURE IT OUT

Tricking people into sharing personal details and passwords by pretending to be someone else—a practice known as phishing—is surprisingly effective. Some of the smartest people I know have been taken in by it and it only takes a moment's lapse in concentration or uncertainty to become a victim. The math is simple: It barely costs anything to send an email to 100,000 people, and only a small fraction of those need to get caught in the net for the effort to pay off.

Scammers have gotten more sophisticated, so look out for targeted spear-phishing attacks in which they may seem to know specific details about you, making their attack more credible. Some scammers even do what's known as whaling—targeting high-profile figures such as heads of companies or celebrities—using elaborately planned and sometimes very convincing schemes.

Consider yourself schooled. Stay vigilant, fellow fish.

SEE ALSO
Two-Factor Authentication, *180*

TYPES OF PHISHING

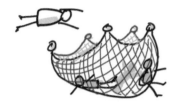

PHISHING

A WIDE NET FOR
CATCHES

SPEAR-PHISHING

INDIVIDUALLY
TARGETED

WHALING

HIGH-PROFILE
TARGETS

 From
amazan.com

Hello,
Please reset
yur account
details.

 From
gofedex.com

Helen,
Your delivery needs
confirmation.

 From
lawyers.con

Dear CEO,
To prevent
legal action...

THE ROAD TO SUCCESS IS DOTTED WITH MANY TEMPTING PARKING SPACES.

— WILL ROGERS

This simple model for the progression of ideas is sometimes called a dialectic. It has deep philosophical roots, but regardless, it's a nice way to think of how ideas—and perhaps society—can progress.

First, something is created or asserted: the thesis. It has some benefits but also some negative effects—the antithesis—that cause us to look for a resolution—synthesis. That new solution then becomes the basis for the next step.

In engineering, I learned that we progress through the resolution of contradictions. As a very simple example, it's nice to have a walking stick. But a full-length walking stick can be awkward to transport. You want it to be long when you're walking but short when you're traveling with it. So we invent retractable ones. But retractable ones break more easily, so we invent...and so on.

SEE ALSO
The Spectrum Policy, *72*
Idempotence, *112*

THESIS, ANTITHESIS, SYNTHESIS

A PROGRESSION OF IDEAS

DING! DING!

DING!

THESIS

A NEW IDEA

 TENSION

ANTITHESIS

AN OPPOSING REACTION

|
RESOLUTION

SYNTHESIS

THE TENSION GETS RESOLVED

and becomes the start of the new thesis...

On the spring and autumn equinoxes, there are almost exactly 12 hours of daylight and 12 hours of night, with the sun rising almost due east and setting due west. The equinoxes mark the halfway point in the sun's ascent to its summer highs and descent into wintry lows.

Technically, the equinox is the instant that the plane of Earth's equator passes through the center of the sun. This usually happens around March 20 for the vernal equinox (spring equinox) and September 23 for the autumnal equinox (fall equinox). Because of the renewal and change associated with the equinoxes, some cultures use them to mark their new year. They officially mark the astronomical change of seasons for the arrival of spring and autumn.

EQUINOX

Aequus Nox — EQUAL NIGHT

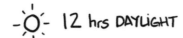 12 hrs DAYLIGHT

RISES DUE
EAST

● 12 hrs NIGHT

SETS DUE
WEST

WINTER → SPRING   and   SUMMER → AUTUMN

Since I learned this trick, I almost look forward to getting a wobbly table at a café if only for the chance to retest this simple, yet still remarkable, fix. It works for a four-legged table with legs of even length that touch the ground in a square on uneven, but not excessively bumpy ground. A number of smart people have spent a surprising amount of time demonstrating that you can fix the wobble by rotating the table up to a quarter turn.

If you have a square-topped table, not a round one, or, say, two square tables next to each other, it's not always possible to start rearranging the café. But when you can, it's really neat to see it work. Give it a try.

SEE ALSO
How to Win at Monopoly, *16*
How to Peel a Sticky Note, *194*

FIX WOBBLY TABLES

A SIMPLE ROTATION IS ALL IT NEEDS

1 RESIST
A FOLDED NAPKIN
UNDER THE LEG

2 ROTATE
UP TO $\frac{1}{4}$ TURN

3 RELAX
AS THE LEGS FIND
A STABLE SPOT

There's an all-you-can-eat buffet with all the flavors of the world and you can have whatever you want. This is going to be amazing! You love lasagna, but look at those fajitas. You go for the fajitas, but then your friend comes back to the table with sushi, which looks even better. Why didn't you get that?? You always screw up.

According to psychologist Barry Schwartz, more choice doesn't always help us choose better and can even make us feel worse about what we chose, even if it was great. Reduced satisfaction arises from:

- Escalation of expectations
- The opportunity cost of all the good options we could have had
- Regret or anticipated regret of our choice
- Self-blame when we think we are responsible for not doing as well as we could have

SEE ALSO
The Coastline Paradox, *14*
The Supporters' Paradox, *270*

THE PARADOX OF CHOICE

TOO MUCH CHOICE LEADS TO PARALYSIS AND DISSATISFACTION

Wow! This has got to be good.

RAISED EXPECTATIONS

Look at all those other flavors

OPPORTUNITY COST

I should've gotten the other one

ANTICIPATED REGRET

I never pick the best one

SELF-BLAME

Good design effortlessly directs attention to what matters while downplaying what doesn't. In this way, the best design and writing shares everything they need to with arresting clarity and minimal fluff.

Many an interface, flier or layout has benefited from a healthy dose of cutting what's already evident. Common candidates for culling are labels attached to forms of data that are self-evident without introduction. These often include email addresses, phone numbers, dates and prices, and, with the right context, may extend to authors, addresses and more. We don't need someone to tell us that contact@joesplumbing.com is an email address, nor that the string of numbers next to it is a phone number.

It's not a blanket rule—good design needs careful consideration of audience and context—but it's a simple step to making the information you want to shine come to the fore.

SEE ALSO
The Golden Ratio, *128*
The 60-30-10 Color Rule, *166*

LET YOUR DATA SPEAK FOR ITSELF

INSTEAD OF

TRY

PARTY!
Date: JULY 27 2024
Email: rsvp@party.com
Tel: 510 123 4567
Cost: $15 entry

PARTY!
JULY 27 2024
rsvp@party.com
510 123 4567
$15 entry

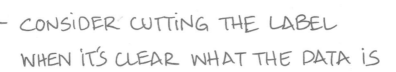

CONSIDER CUTTING THE LABEL
WHEN IT'S CLEAR WHAT THE DATA IS

Life on a nuclear submarine has some pretty intense constraints. For one, there's no natural fresh water, and any time you use water, wastewater builds up in the tanks. The wastewater then has to be expelled, which makes noise, and because nuclear subs don't want to give away their location, they minimize the number of times they do that. That means taking extreme care with the fresh water.

The other reason to take care of the fresh water, which is used for cooking, cleaning and drinking, is that fresh water must be made from seawater. If you drink a glass of water on board, it's probably the most expensive glass of water you'll ever have because it's been desalinated by a nuclear submarine.

Hence, the submarine shower uses a total of 20 seconds of water: 10 seconds with the water on, then water off to soap up and scrub, followed by 10 seconds of rinsing. That's it. For me, it's a nice reframe for how much water you actually need when you take a shower, and it absolutely works. If you fancy saving water and energy, give it a try.

SEE ALSO
Wishcycling, *56*
An Idling Car, *142*

SUBMARINE SHOWER

SHOWER LIKE YOU'RE ON A NUCLEAR SUB

1

WET

10 secs WATER

2

SOAP + SCRUB

WATER OFF

3

RINSE

10 secs WATER

🕐 20 secs WATER TOTAL

We've all been there. You're holding some packaging that kind of looks like it ought to be recyclable but isn't one of the standard products shown in the guidance. You optimistically hope that tossing it in the recycling bin instead of the trash might give it a chance to be recycled. This is known as wishcycling, and, unfortunately, it's not the most helpful approach.

When we put non-recyclables in the recycling bin, they contaminate the high-quality recyclable materials and several things can happen:

- A lot of dry recycling is still manually sorted. When the quality of the input decreases, it requires more people to sort it, which is more expensive.
- Non-recyclable items can damage processing machines that aren't designed for them.
- Contaminated recycling can mean a lower-quality end product.

So, the experts' advice is: Check what you can recycle locally, and if in doubt, keep it out.

SEE ALSO
An Idling Car, *142*
Pollution is Highly Localized, *146*

WISHCYCLING

HOPING SOMETHING CAN BE RECYCLED

INTENTION

HMM, MAYBE IT CAN?

EFFECT

YUCK! WHAT IS THIS??

THE QUALITY'S AWFUL, WE CAN'T SELL IT AND IT'S COSTING TOO MUCH TO SORT

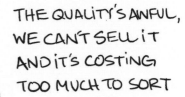

 ✔ CHECK WHAT YOU CAN RECYCLE LOCALLY

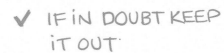 ✔ IF IN DOUBT KEEP IT OUT

This acronym is a handy checklist for considering and clarifying roles and responsibilities. A table detailing the role each person plays for each task is called a Responsibility Assignment Matrix. Somewhat counterintitively, sometimes making it clear who doesn't have a say, rather than who does, can be the most helpful thing to do. The roles break down like this:

RESPONSIBLE

Who will actually be responsible for doing the task.

ACCOUNTABLE

Who is accountable for it being completed.

CONSULTED

Whose opinion will be sought for the task, though they won't be doing it themselves.

INFORMED

Who doesn't get a say in the task but will be kept informed of progress.

SEE ALSO
MoSCoW Prioritization, *184*
The Conscious Competence Learning Model, *218*

The concept of the third teacher means that a well-designed environment can help us learn, encourage good habits and improve our well-being. It applies just as well in an office as in an elementary school. I remember a previous mentor of mine saying he could tell how a project was doing just by taking in the project room. A well-designed environment can helps us learn, fosters creativity, encourages good habits and improves our well-being. It applies just as well in an office as in an elementary school. I remember a mentor of mine saying he could tell how a project was doing just by taking in the project room. However, the design of our online spaces is still catching up with the best that a classroom or project room can achieve.

SEE ALSO
Proxemics, *136*
The Diderot Effect, *234*

THE THIRD TEACHER

A WELL-DESIGNED LEARNING ENVIRONMENT

1 FIRST TEACHER
  TEACHER or PARENT

2 SECOND TEACHER
  PEERS

3 THIRD TEACHER
  ENVIRONMENT

All maps involve decisions. Whenever you compress real life onto something smaller and less detailed, you have to choose what to keep in and what to leave out. In the case of printing a map of Earth, you have to figure out how to get something curved onto something flat, which involves trade-offs and tough decisions. Three-dimensional space just doesn't flatten into two-dimensional paper without choices.

In 1569, Gerardus Mercator created a map that brilliantly solved a pressing problem—that of being able to follow a straight line while sailing and have it correspond to a straight line on the map. His map also did a good job of preserving the shape of countries. But to preserve those shapes, you have to stretch the areas at the top and bottom of Earth. Because most of the land on Earth is in the Northern Hemisphere, and because that land is generally farther north than the land in the Southern Hemisphere is south, the Mercator projection has the effect of enlarging Northern countries such as Europe, the U.S., Canada, Scandinavia and Russia as compared to countries closer to the equator and in the Southern Hemisphere.

To this day, most world maps you see are similar to Mercator's projection. It could well be that this distorts our worldview by emphasizing northern countries in size and therefore importance.

SEE ALSO
The Continental Axis Hypothesis, *116*

MERCATOR PROJECTION

THE 1569 WORLD MAP MADE FOR NAVIGATION

1 THE EARTH IS CURVED

2 WHICH MAKES IT TRICKY TO GET FLAT

IT JUST WON'T EASILY GO FLAT

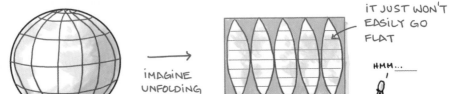

IMAGINE UNFOLDING

HMM...

3 MERCATOR'S MAP WAS GREAT FOR NAVIGATION

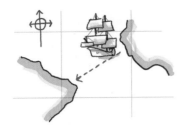

4 AT THE EXPENSE OF ENLARGING NORTH AND SOUTH

STRETCH

5 BECAUSE MOST LAND IS IN THE NORTH THIS MAKES NORTHERN COUNTRIES SEEM LARGER AND PERHAPS MORE IMPORTANT

☐ GREENLAND
☐ AFRICA

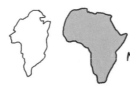

MERCATOR

ACTUAL

Not all of us can ditch jobs, families and responsibilities to go on an adventure, spending the next few months biking around China or trekking across a tundra somewhere. But, as Alastair Humphreys argues in his book *Microadventures*, we don't need anything of that scale to get a perspective-shifting break from the daily grind and make a connection with nature—we can try a microadventure instead. A microadventure might be as simple as setting up camp in the garden with your family; paddling down a local river and camping on the bank; or staying the night on a nearby hilltop under the stars, catching the sunrise and taking a swim in something other than a pool to wake up before making your way back home in time for breakfast.

The essence of a microadventure is that it can be short, simple, local and cheap. No fancy gear, complex planning, big budgets or long travel necessary. An achievable adventure for normal people without giving up the rest of our lives to enjoy it.

SEE ALSO
The 10 Essentials for Wilderness Safety, *154*
The Three-Day Effect, *230*

MiCROADVENTURE
A SHORT, SiMPLE, LOCAL, CHEAP ADVENTURE
LiKE CAMPiNG
OUT ON A
SCHOOLNiGHT

A lot of us may have felt pressure at times to find our purpose—our one true cause, our personal mission, what we personally should be doing and where we fit in. I like this framework and approach from Priya Singh, who suggests we don't have one singular "why"—that our "why" may change often. It's not a pot of gold or treasure to be found.

She shares a framework of three types of work:
1. Work that feeds you and those who depend on you
2. Work that feeds the world
3. Work that feeds your soul

Any work you do may fit into one or more of these, but don't fall into the trap of thinking your work needs to overlap all three. We're each capable of many different projects in our lives, and work that fits into just one or two of these is plenty. Rather than aim for the trap of the one elusive dream job, consider diversifying and satisfying each of these with different activities or at different times.

When presented with an opportunity or an idea, instead of asking why do it, try asking why not. Practice not rejecting yourself before you've even started.

SEE ALSO
Hope, *70*
Nine-Enders, *226*

FIND YOUR "WHY NOT?"

TRY ASKING "WHY NOT?" TO EACH OPPORTUNITY

WORK THAT
FEEDS
ME

+ dependants

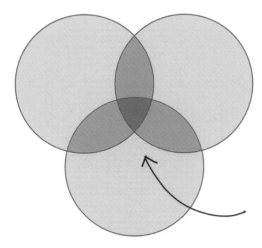

WORK THAT
FEEDS
THE WORLD

WORK THAT FEEDS
MY SOUL

Don't fall into
the trap:

One job doesn't
have to satisfy
all three.
Diversify!

I hadn't given much thought to hope, beyond it being a nice feeling to have, until I discovered Professor Charles R. Snyder's cognitive model for hope, which shed new light on the concept. He proposes a model of hope in which an individual can be hopeful if they have:

1. Goals
If you don't or can't picture any future state you'd like, then you won't have a lot of hope.

2. Pathways
You need to see some ways that you can make step-by-step progress toward your goal.

3. Willpower or Agency
You need to be motivated and believe you can succeed at your goal.

If you're missing any of these, you'll find that hope will be in short supply.

SEE ALSO
Flow, *106*
The Role of a Finishing Line, *274*

HOPE
MORE THAN A FEELING

To feel hopeful you need...

1. GOALS
   A DESIRED FUTURE STATE
   TO AIM FOR

2. PATHWAYS
   SEEING DIFFERENT WAYS
   TO YOUR GOALS

3. WILLPOWER
   BELIEF IN YOUR AGENCY
   AND ABILITY TO SUCCEED

I can do this

Remove any of
these and hope
is diminished

One of my favorite books is a dog-eared 1970 edition of *The Practice of Creativity* by George Prince. The book gives wonderful examples and tools for successful creative discussions in meetings. According to Prince, so much hinges on genuinely listening to and trying to understand others' points of view while creating a space to protect the egos of the participants and an atmosphere of psychological safety. One simple tool he offers is the Spectrum Policy.

The Spectrum Policy acknowledges that few ideas come out fully formed or solve a problem perfectly in one go. Often, our first reaction to hearing something is to evaluate it. When we hear a new idea, we can't help but see the negative aspects—the parts that obviously won't work—and because of these negative aspects, we may dismiss the whole idea. When this happens, not only does the group lose out on what may have been the genesis of a solution, the originator can often feel snubbed and remove themselves from full participation in the rest of the meeting.

The Spectrum Policy recognizes that "because you are never dealing with fools," all ideas put forward, even if we see obvious flaws, have some good points as well as bad. Before pointing out the flaws, make a point of finding and acknowledging the good in an idea. This keeps elements of the idea available for others to build on and preserves the egos of participants, keeping everyone fully engaged in solving the problem.

THE SPECTRUM POLICY

PRACTICE FINDING THE GOOD IN IDEAS

LET'S USE
BUBBLES!

| THEY'LL
JUST POP.

 BUBBLES ARE CHEAP AND
A GREAT INSULATOR.
HOW COULD WE GET THOSE
WITH MORE RESILIENCE?

 IDEAS AS
BLACK OR WHITE

>

 IDEAS AS
A SPECTRUM

The Norse gods are still among us! At least in the names of the days of the week. While Saturday, Sunday and Monday are named for the celestial bodies Saturn, the sun and the moon, the rest of the week is a tribute to Norse mythology:

Tuesday—from Old English Tiw, for Týr, the Norse god of combat
Wednesday—from Old English Woden, for Odin, the one-eyed king of the gods
Thursday—for Thor, the proud god with his magical hammer Mjöllnir
Friday—for Frigg, wife of Odin and goddess of marriage and motherhood

These Norse gods were Germanic language analogs for the original planetary names and corresponding Roman/Greek gods: Mars/Ares (gods of war like Týr), Mercury/Hermes, Jupiter/Zeus, Venus/Aphrodite. In many European languages, the weekdays still bear closer relation to these originals. For example, Monday through Friday in French/Spanish are lundi/lunes, mardi/martes, mercredi/miércoles, jeudi/jueves and vendredi/viernes.

SEE ALSO
Solar System Sizes, *12*
Halloween, *88*

DAYS OF THE WEEK

THE NORSE GODS AMONG US

SATURDAY SUNDAY

MONDAY

TUESDAY
TYR
tiw
from old English

WEDNESDAY
ODIN
woden

THURSDAY
THOR

FRIDAY
FRIGG

It's common knowledge that an acronym is made by taking the initial letters of a set of words and putting them together. So Random Access Memory becomes RAM, and the United States of America becomes the USA. But I only found out recently that these two examples are actually different from each other. In fact, U.S.A. is an initialism!

An acronym is typically when the first letter or letters of a set of words are said as a word, like laser (light amplification by stimulated emission of radiation), radar (radio detection and ranging), sonar (sound navigation and ranging), NATO (North Atlantic Treaty Organization) or NASA (National Aeronautics and Space Administration).

An initialism, by contrast, is when a set of initials are pronounced as letters when you say them, like FBI, CIA, USA, BBC or CD.

SEE ALSO
How To Speak Plainly, *120*

ACRONYM

SAID AS A WORD

Light amplification by stimulated emission of radiation

laser

pronounced by

SAYING THE WORD

laser

\ˈlā-zər\

INITIALISM

SAID AS LETTERS

Federal Bureau of Investigation

FBI

pronounced by

SPELLING OUT THE LETTERS

F B I

\ˈef\ \ˈbē\ \ˈī\

Astronauts returning from space have repeatedly shared experiences like this:

> *"You develop an instant global consciousness, a people orientation, an intense dissatisfaction with the state of the world, and a compulsion to do something about it. From out there on the moon, international politics look so petty."*
>
> —Edgar Mitchell, Apollo 14 astronaut

Or this:

> *"When we look down at the earth from space, we see this amazing, indescribably beautiful planet. It looks like a living, breathing organism. But it also, at the same time, looks extremely fragile…. Anybody else who's ever gone to space says the same thing because it really is striking and it's really sobering to see this paper-thin layer and to realize that that little paper-thin layer is all that protects every living thing on Earth from death, basically. From the harshness of space."*
>
> —Ron Garan, ISS astronaut

The overview effect, coined by Frank White, is the ultimate version of seeing the forest for the trees. It's the realization that we live on a fragile planet, we are all connected and this is all we've got.

THE OVERVIEW EFFECT

THE REALIZATION THAT THIS IS ALL WE'VE GOT

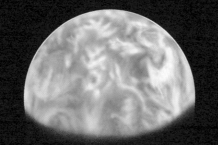

If you're a pretty dedicated reader, you may be able to get through one book a week, so roughly 50 books a year. Over 70 years of reading at that pace, you'd read around 3,500 books—counting comfort rereads like *Harry Potter*. I only know a few people who actually manage to read like that, so presumably, for most of us, the number we will manage is much smaller.

To put that number in context, your local bookstore likely has around 30,000 books. So if you were to use your entire life's reading in that store, you'd still only be a bit over one-tenth of the way through. That's a lot of books you didn't even get a chance to start. In fact, In the course of making this sketch, I learned that in 2010 the Google Books team estimated there were around 130 million books to choose from.

I won't deny that 3,500 books in a lifetime is a lot, but whatever you do, there will be far more books that you just don't have time to read than those you do find time for. So, as with movies, I think it's wise to be at least a little thoughtful about what books you choose to pick up, and what books you decide to finish.

SEE ALSO
Tsundoku, *238*
The Shapes of Stories, *250*

HOW MANY BOOKS CAN YOU READ IN A LIFETIME?

LET'S SAY YOU READ A LOT

I BOOK
A WEEK

50 BOOKS
A YEAR

that's

3,500 BOOKS
OVER 70 YEARS

OUR LOCAL BOOKSTORE HAS ROUGHLY **30,000** BOOKS

CHOOSE WISELY.

MINDS

ARE LIKE

PARACHUTES.

THEY ONLY FUNCTION
WHEN THEY ARE OPEN.

— Commonly attributed to Thomas Dewar

Remarkably, when we describe a noun, we almost always unconsciously arrange adjectives in this order: opinion, size, age, shape, color, origin, material, purpose.

If you try mixing them up in a different order, it just doesn't sound right. Compare, for example, a super little Italian coffee to an Italian little super coffee. Or, as Mark Forsyth points out in *The Elements of Eloquence: How to Turn the Perfect English Phrase*, you can have a great green dragon, but not a green great one.

SEE ALSO
How to Speak Plainly, *120*

ORDERING ADJECTIVES

ENGLISH ADJECTIVES ALMOST ALWAYS FOLLOW THIS ORDER

The biggest killer of houseplants? Overwatering. I love this simple tip known as the finger-dip test, or the knuckle test, to determine if your typical houseplant needs watering. Sadly, it came too late for many of my plants, but perhaps not for yours.

Just dip your index finger into the soil near the stem of your plant up to about your first knuckle. If the soil feels dry and your finger comes out clean, then it's time for some water. If the soil feels moist, then it's time to sit back next to your plant with a good book and enjoy it.

SEE ALSO
Autumn Leaves, 90
Animals That Regenerate, *186*

THE FINGER-DIP TEST

TO HELP NOT OVERWATER HOUSEPLANTS

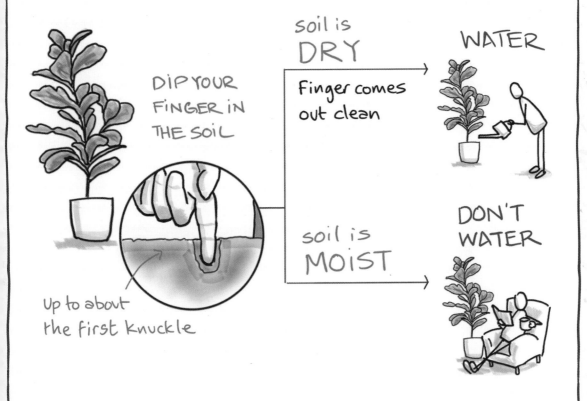

DIP YOUR FINGER IN THE SOIL

Up to about the first knuckle

soil is **DRY**
Finger comes out clean

WATER

soil is **MOIST**

DON'T WATER

Perhaps when you first dressed up as a ghost and went to houses asking for candy, you paused to wonder what the meaning of Halloween was. If, like me, you didn't, read on. Halloween is a blend of "hallow," Old English for "saint," and "e'en," a contraction of "even," meaning "eve." So it's really the night before All Hallows or All Saints' Day on November 1, the day when Christians celebrate the lives of past saints and martyrs. It's also part of the season of events called Allhallowtide including All Souls' Day on November 2.

The other Halloween traditions come from a mix of sources over hundreds of years that are both complex and somewhat disputed. I like that the jack o'lantern, before transferring itself to a pumpkin in the U.S., was originally carved out of a turnip.

SEE ALSO
Equinox, *46*
Days of the Week, *74*

THE NIGHT BEFORE ALL SAINTS' DAY

HALLOWEEN

SAINT
From Old English "Holy"

EVE
from Scots "even"

31 OCT | 1 NOV | 2 NOV
HALLOWEEN | ALL SAINTS' DAY | ALL SOULS' DAY

← ———————— Allhallowtide ————————→

What a lovely time of year—when the leaves of deciduous trees in many forests change from the deep greens of summer to the yellows, oranges and reds of fall. But what makes the leaves change color and what compounds are responsible for nature's spectacular display?

Many of us will know the green of chlorophyll, but leaves also contain carotenoids. As the chlorophyll fades, the golden oranges of these carotenoids start to shine through. You may recognize one carotenoid, beta-carotene, from carrots. Another carotenoid, xanthophyll, is responsible for the beautiful bright yellows. The leaves of some trees also produce anthocyanin as autumn begins, which produces those striking deep reds.

SEE ALSO
Seasons, 32
The Three-Day Effect, *230*

AUTUMN LEAVES

AND THE COMPOUNDS THAT CAUSE THEIR COLORS

CHLOROPHYLL

XANTHOPHYLL

CAROTENOIDS

ANTHOCYANIN

THAT SPRING
AND SUMMER
GREEN

A CAROTENOID.
BEAUTIFUL YELLOW
AS CHLOROPHYLL
FADES

ABSORB GREEN +
BLUE. REFLECT
RED + YELLOW
= GOLDEN ORANGE

AS AUTUMN STARTS.
RANGES FROM
REDS TO BLUES
BASED ON ACIDITY

The phrase "Solvitur Ambulando" translates more or less to "it is solved by walking." And, indeed, there is something about walking that helps both clear the mind and think clearly. Charles Darwin had a "thinking path" he used to walk daily. Henry David Thoreau wrote a book on walking, and Thomas Jefferson wrote about its value in relaxing the mind. Perhaps that's why a walk can be just what's needed to get a different perspective when you've been sitting at your desk banging your head against a problem.

SEE ALSO
The Third Teacher, 62
The Three-Day Effect, *230*

The rule of thirds is a simple technique to help compose a photograph or layout in a way that's aesthetically pleasing and draws interest. To use it, divide the horizontal and vertical into thirds and aim to place primary elements of the composition at the intersections. When constructed this way, a picture has a clear focus while letting your eye make the most of the whole scene.

The rule of thirds bears a great deal of similarity to the golden ratio, and you can see it in action back to paintings from the Renaissance. You'll even find the view from your phone camera can display grid lines in thirds to make it a breeze to try in your photos.

SEE ALSO
Atmospheric Perspective, *18*
The Golden Ratio, *128*

THE RULE OF THIRDS
FOR COMPOSING PHOTOGRAPHS

KEY FEATURES
AT INTERSECTIONS

HORIZON ON
A THIRD

Phase transitions are the process of changing from one state of matter to another. When an ice cube melts it becomes a liquid; when water freezes it becomes ice. It's typical for solids to transition to liquids and liquids to transition to gases but some transitions skip those steps. Sublimation is when a solid transitions directly to a gas, and deposition is when a gas transitions directly to a solid. Some transitions have their own subtleties, for example, vaporization is evaporation when it's below boiling point and occurring at the surface of a liquid, yet boiling occurs below the surface of a liquid when it's above boiling point.

While we rarely encounter it in our everyday lives, a fourth state of matter, plasma, is both abundant in the universe and the dominant form of the gases in the Sun.

SEE ALSO
The Goldilocks Zone, *174*
The Potato Radius, *214*

STATES OF MATTER
AND THE PHASE TRANSITIONS BETWEEN THEM

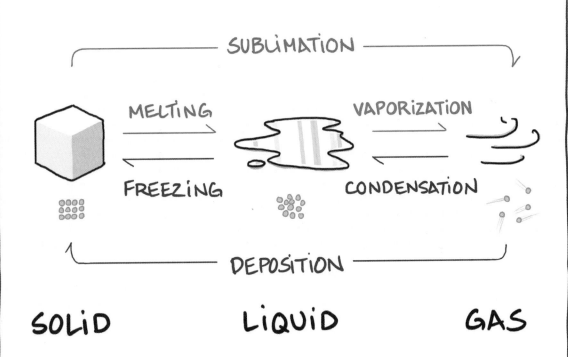

SOLID   LIQUID   GAS

'THE CAT SAT ON THE MAT'
is not a story.

'THE CAT SAT ON THE DOG'S MAT'

is a story.

—JOHN LE CARRÉ

Always almost due north, the Pole Star or North Star (Polaris) is a navigator's best friend. To find it, follow the two stars on the end of the cup in the Big Dipper—part of the constellation Ursa Major or Great Bear—to the most prominent star. The North Star happens to be the last star in the tail of the Little Dipper—the constellation Ursa Minor or the Little Bear. Handy for a navigation sanity check at night.

The North Star is the star that stays fixed in those neat star trail photos in which all the other stars rotate in a circle as the Earth turns.

SEE ALSO
The 10 Essentials for Wilderness Safety, *154*
Know Your Clouds, *164*

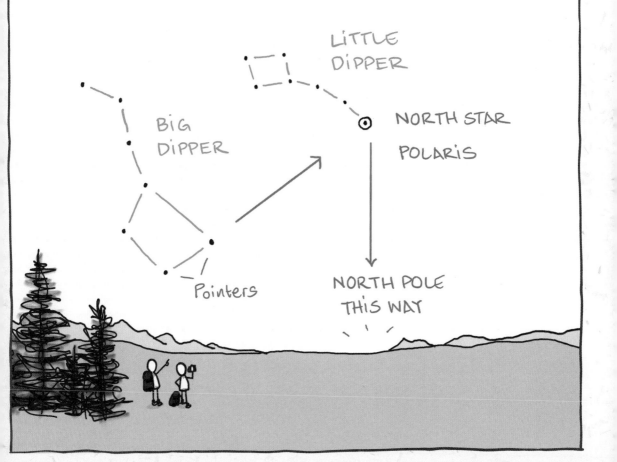

Unlike the Northern Hemisphere, where you can use Polaris, the North Star, to determine which way is north, there's no obvious star that indicates south in the Southern Hemisphere. Instead, you have to use two handy indicators: the Southern Cross—easily spotted, fortunately—and two stars known as The Pointers. Find where these intersect, and you've found due south.

Or, if you prefer, you can follow the direction the Southern Cross is pointing for a distance equal to 4.5 times the length of the constellation to arrive at the spot.

I wondered about reliable methods of identifying south in the Northern Hemisphere and north in the Southern Hemisphere. The simple answer is to find north or south and turn around. Incidentally, you'll find the five main stars of the Southern Cross, or Crux, in prime position on the Australian flag.

SEE ALSO
Mercator Projection, *64*
The Continental Axis Hypothesis, *116*

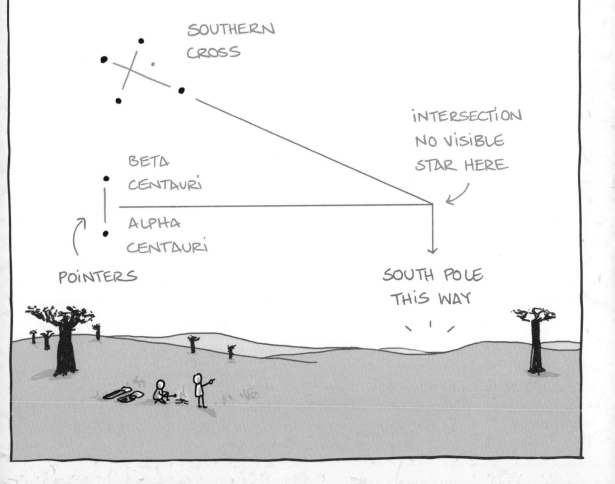

Some simple wisdom from Kurt Vonnegut: Notice when you're happy.

"My uncle Alex Vonnegut, a Harvard-educated life insurance salesman who lived at 5033 North Pennsylvania Street, taught me something very important. He said that when things were really going well we should be sure to NOTICE it. He was talking about simple occasions, not great victories: maybe drinking lemonade on a hot afternoon in the shade, or smelling the aroma of a nearby bakery; or fishing, and not caring if we catch anything or not, or hearing somebody all alone playing a piano really well in the house next door. Uncle Alex urged me to say this out loud during such epiphanies: If this isn't nice, I don't know what is."

Reflecting on this lesson, Vonnegut writes, "So I do the same now, and so do my kids and grandkids. And I urge you to please notice when you are happy, and exclaim or murmur or think at some point, 'If this isn't nice, I don't know what is.'"

SEE ALSO
The Shapes of Stories, *250*
The Supporters' Paradox, *270*

Ever since I came across psychologist Mihaly Csikszentmihalyi's concept of flow, it has stayed with me as a simple framework and beacon for finding joy, creativity and total involvement with life.

When in flow, people are wholly focused on the present moment. They experience a strong sense of control, lose their self-consciousness and ego and their experience of the passage of time changes so that time can fly by or a moment can seem to slow down. Plus, the joy of performing the activity becomes an end in itself.

Flow has a fairly simple set of conditions that I find myself using as a little mental checklist:

1. Clear goals
2. Clear feedback about progress
3. Situations where the challenge of an activity is the right level for my skills

SEE ALSO
The Conscious Competence Learning Model, *218*

FLOW

STATE OF TOTAL FOCUS AND JOY

Conditions for Flow

1. CLEAR GOALS
   AN AiM iN MiND

2. FEEDBACK
   SEE YOUR PROGRESS

3. CHALLENGE MATCHED
   TO SKiLLS
   GROW AND LEARN

In flow
THE ACTIVITY BECOMES
AN END IN iTSELF

focused on
the present

Sense of
control

transformation
of time

loss of
self-consciousness

Lake Effect Snow is a phenomenon where crazy amounts of snow can fall during massive storms on a lake's downwind—leeward—side. Where the effect is pronounced, to the east of some of the Great Lakes in the U.S. (think Buffalo) for example, it's responsible for the region known as the snow belt.

It works like this: Cold air blows over a lake. As the cold air passes over the warmer lake, it picks up water vapor from the lake, which warms the air. This causes the air to rise and, in turn, cool, such that when it reaches the downwind side of the lake, it has become cold and moist. This simple change can lead to some incredible snowstorms dumping 2 to 3 inches of snow per hour.

If there is a rise in land elevation along the path of the cold air, the air can cool faster and increase the effect. And if there's a lot of convection and the air rises quickly, you can even get what's called thundersnow—a thunderstorm in a snowstorm.

SEE ALSO
Seasons, *32*
Know Your Clouds, *164*

LAKE EFFECT SNOW

NATURE'S GREATEST SNOW MACHINE

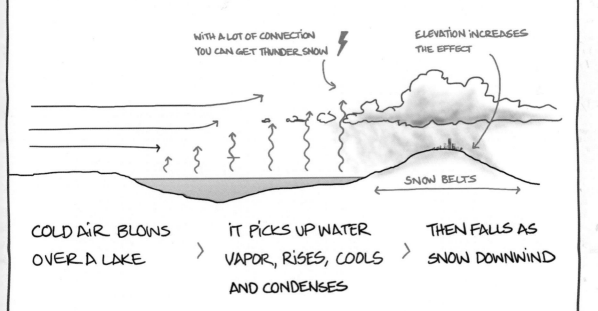

WITH A LOT OF CONVECTION
YOU CAN GET THUNDER SNOW

ELEVATION INCREASES
THE EFFECT

SNOW BELTS

COLD AIR BLOWS
OVER A LAKE

> IT PICKS UP WATER
VAPOR, RISES, COOLS
AND CONDENSES

> THEN FALLS AS
SNOW DOWNWIND

Growing up on the island of Great Britain, I took for granted that after a few hours of travel in most directions, I'd be looking out to sea. But if you were born in a landlocked country you can't reach a coast on the sea without leaving the country.

There are just two countries that are double-landlocked: Uzbekistan and Liechtenstein, a principality located between Switzerland and Austria. Being double-landlocked means that not only are they landlocked with no access to the high seas themselves but they're also surrounded by countries that are themselves landlocked.

Another way to put it is that you have to cross two national boundaries before reaching water connected to the oceans.

SEE ALSO
The Coastline Paradox, *14*
The Traveling Salesman Problem, *38*

DOUBLE-LANDLOCKED

SURROUNDED BY LANDLOCKED COUNTRIES

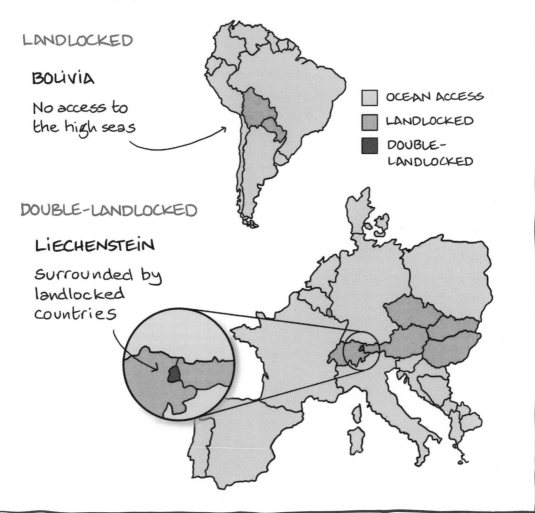

LANDLOCKED

BOLIVIA

No access to
the high seas

OCEAN ACCESS

LANDLOCKED

DOUBLE-
LANDLOCKED

DOUBLE-LANDLOCKED

LIECHENSTEIN

Surrounded by
landlocked
countries

Idempotence essentially describes an operation that, no matter how many times you do it, will still yield the same result, as long as there aren't other operations in between. To give a classic example: *view_your_bank_balance* is idempotent, but *withdraw_1000* is not. It's a property that's often handy since you can retry the operation without worrying about unintended effects.

Idempotence is a concept from mathematics and computer science but can be applied more generally. For example, a simple off button is idempotent, which can be very useful in emergencies as a machine will stay off no matter how many times it is pressed.

SEE ALSO
Decimal vs. Binary, *138*
Yak Shaving, *242*

IDEMPOTENCE

WHEN REPEATING AN OPERATION YIELDS THE SAME RESULT

IDEMPOTENT

LOOK_AT_CAKE

LOOK_AT_CAKE

LOOK_AT_CAKE

LOOK_AT_CAKE

NOT IDEMPOTENT

EAT_SLICE_OF_CAKE

EAT_SLICE_OF_CAKE

EAT_SLICE_OF_CAKE

EAT_SLICE_OF_CAKE

Despite our best efforts or intentions, we have a remarkable history of messing things up in unexpected ways. One simple theory for why this may be is that unintended consequences are likely to happen whenever we try to regulate a complex system by using a simple system. This often happens in any kind of large-scale or government attempt to control a complex system using relatively simple programs, regulations, laws, policies or other actions. No matter how hard we try, there are always unanticipated effects.

Examples abound:

- A policy to suppress forest fires that causes even more fires.
- More open workplaces that cause people to behave more privately.
- Elimination of predators that leads to the proliferation of grazing animals and a reduction in diversity.
- Building a dam affects ecosystems up and down a river.
- What happens when you change software.

Often, the outcome can be the opposite of what you intended, known as the cobra effect. For example, in Bogotá, an attempt to reduce traffic by restricting who could drive each day based on license plates led people to simply buy more cars. Controlling complex systems is difficult.

SEE ALSO
Chesterton's Fence, *232*
Yak Shaving, *242*

THE LAW OF
UNINTENDED CONSEQUENCES

OFTEN SEEN WHEN

A
SIMPLE
SYSTEM — TRIES TO
REGULATE → A
COMPLEX
SYSTEM

ACTION → ?

Jared Diamond's classic book *Guns, Germs, and Steel* proposes some remarkable hypotheses about the pattern of history, notably trying to answer the question of why Europeans generally invaded the rest of the world rather than the other way around. One hypothesis, striking in its simplicity once you take a look at a world map, is the orientation of the major continents.

The Americas are largely lined up north-south, while Europe and Asia (Eurasia) are largely lined up east-west. An east-west alignment means the land is likelier to have a similar climate, day length and seasonal variation. The broad logic of the hypothesis is that the similar latitude of an east-west alignment means animals, crops and humans (through travel and trade) spread across the continents more easily than across those with a north-south alignment—of the Americas and Africa—which naturally encounter different climatic zones.

As a simplified example, horses and other large animals and crops spread throughout the shared temperate latitudes of Eurasia. In contrast, South America's only large domesticated animal, the thick-coated llama (and related species such as the alpaca), couldn't easily spread to North America through the impassable tropical barrier of the Isthmus of Panama. They just aren't built for it.

SEE ALSO
Who Cut Down the Last Tree?, *36*
Mercator Projection, *64*

THE CONTINENTAL AXIS HYPOTHESIS

CROPS, INNOVATIONS AND ANIMALS SPREAD
EAST-WEST MORE EASILY THAN NORTH-SOUTH

NORTH-SOUTH
Americas axis

EAST-WEST
Eurasian axis

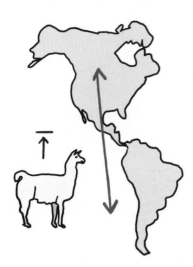

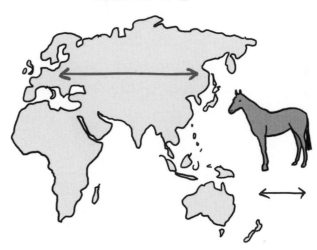

For example

It's harder for llamas
to cross the range of
habitats to N America

...than for horses to
cross the temperate
climate of Eurasia

Despite the implications of various forms of media, there's a crucial, and fascinating distinction between mazes and labyrinths.

A maze is a multi-branched, complex structure with twists, turns, choices, dead-ends and treasure or a Triwizard cup in the center. It's confusing, daunting, exciting, fun, challenging and maybe deadly. A maze heightens awareness, concentration and heart rate.

A labyrinth has a single path. One long, twisting, unwavering path toward the central destination and back out. It's simple, calming, straightforward, reassuring and satisfying. Every step is progress. There are no tough choices to make. No paths, maps or mental models to balance in your head. Nothing to intrude on your thoughts, just your next step. A labyrinth gives space for your thoughts and is calming and peaceful, no matter what David Bowie and Jim Henson have to say about it.

If you want adventure and action, find a maze. If you want calm and contemplation, find a labyrinth.

SEE ALSO
Solvitur Ambulando, *92*
The Three-Day Effect, *230*

MAZE

MANY CHOICES
multicursal

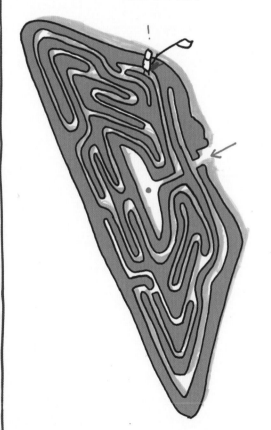

LABYRINTH

SINGLE PATH
unicursal

First published in the 1920s, A.A. Milne's classic children's stories of Winnie-the-Pooh (originally hyphenated) contain a surprising amount of wisdom. If you haven't read them for a long time, you could do much worse than to revisit them. As one small example, as we get older, more and more of us tend to speak like Owl, when we could all probably benefit from a dose of Pooh's simplicity. Owl never uses a short, simple word when a long and complicated one would do. For example, in one revealing exchange, Owl explains, "Well, the customary procedure in such cases is as follows." "What does Crustimoney Proseedcake mean?" responds Pooh. "It means, the Thing to Do," explains Owl.

SEE ALSO
Ordering Adjectives, *84*
The Shapes of Stores, *250*

HOW TO
SPEAK PLAINLY

THE ASCENT IS
PROCEEDING AS
EXPECTED

UP WE GO

OWL-SPEAK

POOH-SPEAK

I grew up with the idea that there are developed countries and developing countries; the "rich" world and the "poor" world. I didn't actively consider this assumption. It's just always been there. And it's wrong.

In his excellent book *Factfulness*, Hans Rosling shows that wealthier countries tend to have smaller families and a low child mortality rate. In contrast, poorer countries are more likely to have larger families and a high child mortality rate. Plotting the spread of countries in the 1960s gives a reasonable approximation of a cluster of "developed" countries with small families where most children survive and a cluster of "developing" countries with larger families where more children die. But that was in the '60s.

The world has changed a lot since then, and that model of dividing the world into two buckets no longer holds true with the data. Instead, Rosling provides a new model to replace it with four income levels instead of two. This distribution better reflects most people's reality, with the vast majority of us somewhere in the middle.

SEE ALSO
Mercator Projection, *64*
The Overview Effect, *78*

A WORLD OF 4 INCOME LEVELS

A DEVELOPED + DEVELOPING WORLDVIEW IS NO LONGER VALID

1965

THE LABELS DEVELOPED + DEVELOPING USED TO FIT NICELY WITH DATA

● size of country

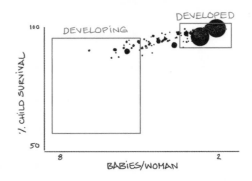

2017

BUT IN 2017 DATA THERE IS NO GAP TO WARRANT A MODEL OF 2 BUCKETS

So here's

A NEW WORLDVIEW

WITH 4 INCOME LEVELS AND MORE PEOPLE IN THE MIDDLE

🧍 Each figure is 1 billion people

PEOPLE VS INCOME/DAY

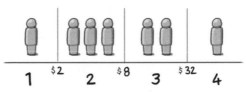

The OODA loop is military strategist John Boyd's framework for combat operations, but it also applies to businesses and learning in general. It emphasizes a rapid cycle of **O**bserving, **O**rienting, **D**eciding and **A**cting.

Though it's not so different from the classic test-learn cycle, Boyd's framework has a lot of nuances. I find it valuable to apply it to my own life because:

1. The faster you can do this loop—in your work or in a conflict of any kind—the more solutions you can try and the quicker you will learn.

2. If you're competing against others, completing your OODA loop fast and acting to change the environment for them means you can disrupt their loop and force them back to the observation step before they can act. It slows them down, creates confusion and gives you an advantage.

SEE ALSO
RACI, *60*
Flow, *106*

THE OODA LOOP

A FRAMEWORK FOR ACTION IN CONFLICT

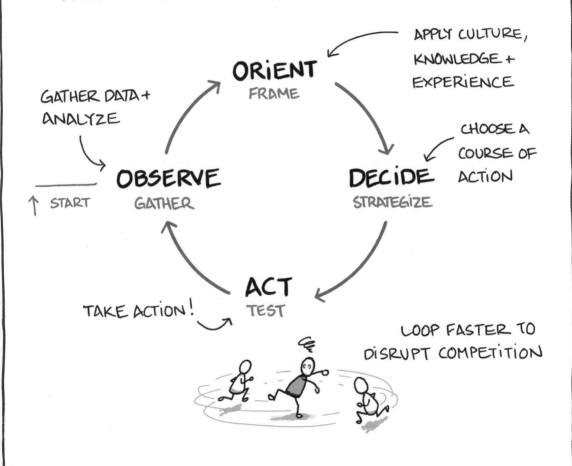

ORIENT
FRAME

APPLY CULTURE,
KNOWLEDGE +
EXPERIENCE

GATHER DATA +
ANALYZE

OBSERVE
GATHER

↑ START

CHOOSE A
COURSE OF
ACTION

DECIDE
STRATEGIZE

ACT
TEST

TAKE ACTION!

LOOP FASTER TO
DISRUPT COMPETITION

GOOD JUDGMENT
COMES FROM EXPERIENCE,

AND EXPERIENCE COMES FROM
BAD JUDGMENT.

— POPULAR WISDOM

The proportions of the golden ratio have been studied and pondered over by mathematicians since the Ancient Greeks. It's a handy shortcut to make something we find innately pleasing. The formula creates an aspect ratio and repeating subdivisions where the ratio of the long over the short segment is the same as both added together over the long segment.

The golden ratio pops up in all sorts of places. It's found in the pyramids, the Parthenon, the Mona Lisa, violins, photography and, very deliberately, in corporate logos. In nature, the golden spiral abounds in the shell of the nautilus, the spiral of strawberry seeds, the spikes of cacti and the swirl of hurricanes. No wonder it's sometimes called the golden ratio of beauty.

SEE ALSO
The Rule of Thirds, *94*
One-Point Perspective, *202*

THE GOLDEN RATIO

PLEASING PROPORTIONS FOUND IN NATURE

THE RATIO
WHERE

$$\frac{LONG}{SHORT} = \frac{LONG + SHORT}{LONG} = 1.618$$

FOR
EXAMPLE

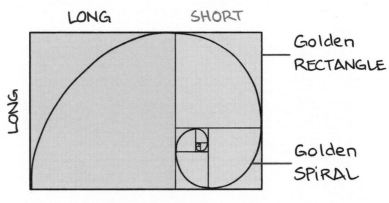

LONG   SHORT

LONG

Golden
RECTANGLE

Golden
SPIRAL

LONG + SHORT

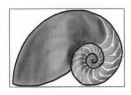

NATURE

ARCHITECTURE

ART

From the teeniest, tiniest shrew weighing just a few grams to the largest whale—including animals as diverse as robins, monkeys, sea lions and giraffes—a typical mammal's heart will beat roughly 1.5 billion times over the course of its expected life.

What's more, simply knowing a mammal's weight helps predict several other fundamental aspects of its life. Tiny mammals tend to have hearts that go like crazy. They live briefly and reach maturity quickly. Large animals, in contrast, have slow heart rates, long lives and take longer to reach adulthood.

The most significant outlier is humanity, largely because, in recent years, we've significantly extended our lifetime from what would be expected from nature.

SEE ALSO
Nurse Log, *28*
The Square-Cube Law, *140*

1·5 BILLION HEARTBEATS

MAMMALS SHARE ROUGHLY THE SAME HEARTBEATS IN A LIFETIME

From the tiny
SHREW

to the mighty
ELEPHANT

↑ HEART RATE   ~ 1500 bpm
↓ LIFE SPAN   2 years

↓ HEART RATE   ~ 30 bpm
↑ LIFE SPAN   75 years

NUMBER OF BEATS IN A LIFETIME

10^{10} 10^9 10^8

RAT   CAT   DOG   HORSE   ELEPHANT

10 10^2 10^3 10^4 10^5

MONKEY   PEOPLE   GIRAFFE   WHALE

WEIGHT (kg)

$10^9 = 1,000,000,000$

I like this simple model of self-awareness, where each quadrant is a window into an aspect of your relationship with others. Most people won't be aware of much that you know about yourself—through sharing or disclosure, you help others understand more about you. Conversely, some aspects of you can only be seen by others—you need to receive feedback to learn about these. Still other things about you, especially when you are young, may remain buried in your unconscious mind and are thus unknown to you and others.

For each of our relationships, the relative size of each quadrant may be different. For example, if you start on a new team at work, there will be a lot you need to share with your colleagues to help them understand you better. Your oldest friends, on the other hand, may know how you'll act before you do yourself.

SEE ALSO
The Third Teacher, *62*
The Conscious Competence Learning Model, *218*

JOHARI WINDOW

A WINDOW OF FEEDBACK AND SHARING

	KNOWN TO SELF	UNKNOWN TO SELF
KNOWN TO OTHERS	OPEN SELF You know I love karaoke!	BLIND SPOT There's something on your face
UNKNOWN TO OTHERS	HIDDEN SELF I'm having a hard time at home	UNKNOWN SELF A hidden talent or fear

DISCLOSURE

------- FEEDBACK ⟶

MODEL: PSYCHOLOGISTS JOSEPH LUFT AND HARRY INGHAM

The BS Asymmetry Principle, also known as Brandolini's Law, is the simple observation that it's far easier to produce and spread bullshit, misinformation and nonsense than it is to refute it.

So pervasive is this phenomenon that the iSchool at the University of Washington launched a course called Calling Bullshit. The first class was fully booked within one minute.

Phil Williamson, Associate Professor at the University of East Anglia in the UK, wrote a short article in *Nature* emphasizing that we should take the time and effort to correct misinformation where we can. In it, he proposed the idea that "the global scientific community could...set up its own, moderated, rating system for websites that claim to report on science. We could call it the Scientific Honesty and Integrity Tracker, and give online nonsense the SHAIT rating it deserves."

SEE ALSO
Survivorship Bias, *26*
The Overview Effect, *78*

THE BS ASYMMETRY PRINCIPLE

THE AMOUNT OF ENERGY NEEDED TO REFUTE BS IS AN ORDER OF MAGNITUDE BIGGER THAN TO PRODUCE IT

WAIT! I BET THE MOON'S MADE OF CHEESE.

WELL, SPECTROGRAPHIC ANALYSIS AND ORBIT CALCULATIONS SUGGEST NOT. PLUS, WE BUILT A ROCKET, TOOK PEOPLE THERE, AND THEY COULDN'T EAT IT.

...HM, YEAH I'M STILL THINKING CHEESE.

EFFORT

EFFORT

AKA BRANDOLINI'S LAW

Distinct from ergonomics, which is more about how people fit into their environment, proxemics focuses on the social aspect of space. For example: At what distance are you intimate? Where does your personal space end? How far away should you be for an honest discussion? Why are big circular wedding and conference tables so frustrating for conversations? How close should desks be in an office to encourage collaboration without feeling jammed together?

A colleague of mine used to give a fine example. Folks will whisper politely and with awe under the high vaulted ceilings of a cathedral, while the confession booth is low and close: more comfortable for sharing your deepest secrets. An olde English pub that you have to stoop to enter immediately feels friendly and intimate. In contrast, you'll struggle to have a deep conversation in a warehouse.

SEE ALSO
Maze vs. Labyrinth, *118*
The Four Horsemen of Relationship Apocalypse, *160*

PROXEMICS
THE SCIENCE OF SOCIAL DISTANCE

for example

HIGH CEILINGS
FEEL COLDER +
IMPERSONAL

LOW CEILINGS
FEEL MORE
INTIMATE

Whisper in a
tall, grand
cathedral...

...but confess
in a tiny
booth

We find it handy to count in the decimal system, using 10 numbers from 0 to 9—also known as base-10. After all, we're born with 10 fingers and toes to count with.

But it turns out you can represent all numbers just as well using only two digits—0 and 1—using a system known as base-2. This is also called the binary system and is credited to Gottfried Wilhelm Leibniz, a 17th-century polymath.

The binary system is handy because 1s and 0s can represent a simple positive/negative value, such as open/closed or on/off. This made binary the choice for designing computers and is how digital information is stored and transmitted today.

Each 0 or 1 in a binary number is known as a bit—coined by Claude Shannon as short for binary digit—and 8 bits is known as a byte.

SEE ALSO
Idempotence, *112*

We use
this

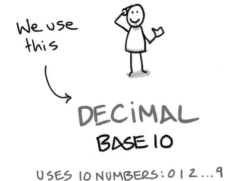

Computers
use this

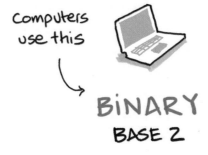

DECIMAL
BASE 10

USES 10 NUMBERS: 0 1 2 ... 9

BINARY
BASE 2

USES 2 NUMBERS: 0 1

$\circ$	$\circ$	1	3

$$10^3 \quad 10^2 \quad 10^1 \quad 10^0$$

$0 \times 1000 \quad 0 \times 100 \quad 1 \times 10 \quad 3 \times 1$

1	1	0	1

$2 \times 2 \times 2$

$$2^3 \quad 2^2 \quad 2^1 \quad 2^0$$

$1 \times 8 \quad 1 \times 4 \quad 0 \times 2 \quad 1 \times 1$

$= 0 + 0 + 10 + 3 = \boxed{13}$

$= 8 + 4 + 0 + 1 = \boxed{13}$

As an adult, I've found myself wondering at how I found the monkey bars in the playground so much easier to swing on as a kid than I do now. The reason is partly to do with the square-cube law.

The square-cube law is a deceptively simple observation: As you scale up an object—say, as you get taller—its area increases in proportion to the square of its dimensions. In contrast, its volume increases in proportion to the cube of its dimensions.

The strength of bones, muscles or wooden beams is proportional to their cross-sectional area—increasing with a square of its width. However, the weight they have to handle increases due to the volume—increasing by the cube of its width. So as size increases, relative strength decreases.

This fundamental relationship has enormous significance when considering the sizes of animals, how big trees can grow, how long bridges can be and numerous other practical questions.

The small size of children relative to the area of their muscles and bones makes them relatively stronger than adults, so they can more easily support their weight as they swing on the monkey bars. The same law makes push-ups harder for larger people. It's also part of the reason short trees can be spindly but big trees have chunkier trunks and why we need increasingly strong materials to build bigger and bigger skyscrapers compared to what you'd need for the shed in your garden.

SEE ALSO
1.5 Billion Heartbeats, *130*
Walking Speeds, *266*

THE SQUARE - CUBE LAW

AND HOW STRENGTH SCALES WITH SIZE

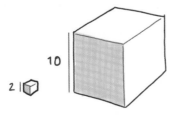

AREA SCALES WITH THE SQUARE OF LENGTH

while

VOLUME SCALES WITH THE CUBE OF LENGTH

LENGTH	2		10	
AREA	4	2^2	100	10^2
VOLUME	8	2^3	1000	10^3

BECAUSE STRENGTH SCALES WITH CROSS-SECTIONAL AREA— of bones, muscles, beams — IT GETS HARDER TO SUPPORT OUR WEIGHT (from volume) AS WE SCALE UP.

chunky trunks

steel beams

RELATIVE STRENGTH DECREASES AS SIZE INCREASES

THIS HELPS EXPLAIN WHY

EASY!

ELEPHANTS NEED CHUNKY LEGS

SPINDLY ANT LEGS CAN SUPPORT 50 ANTS

KIDS ARE BETTER AT MONKEY BARS

An average idling car can produce enough exhaust emissions to fill 150 balloons every minute. That's a lot of balloons puffing out of the cars idling outside a school at pickup time. Other tests have found that for any time over 10 seconds, fuel use and emissions are always greater when idling than when turning off the engine and restarting when ready to go, which is why many newer models of car turn off the engine automatically.

SEE ALSO
Pollution is Highly Localized, *146*

EVERY MINUTE, AN IDLING CAR CAN PRODUCE ENOUGH EXHAUST EMISSIONS TO FILL 150 BALLOONS

Consider turning your engine off.

This simple equation from founder and CEO of Trusted Advisor Associates Charles Green considers what makes someone trustworthy. It breaks down trustworthiness as the sum of a person's credibility, reliability and how intimate or safe they help you feel divided by the self-orientation of the person. You can think of self-orientation as whether they focus their attention more on themselves or if they are genuinely interested in you and your success. Self-interest reduces trustworthiness, while having common goals strengthens it. It's much easier to trust someone when they are qualified, consistently show up, create a safe atmosphere and when you believe their interests align with yours.

SEE ALSO
The BS Asymmetry Principle, *134*
Trust Battery, *224*

THE TRUST EQUATION

 THEY KNOW THEIR STUFF

 THEY ALWAYS DELIVER

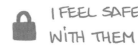 I FEEL SAFE WITH THEM

$$\text{TRUST} = \frac{\underset{\text{CREDIBILITY}}{C} + \underset{\text{RELIABILITY}}{R} + \underset{\text{INTIMACY}}{I}}{\underset{\text{SELF-ORIENTATION}}{S}}$$

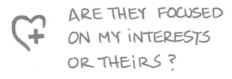 ARE THEY FOCUSED ON MY INTERESTS OR THEIRS?

Sure, the big city is worse than the country for air quality. But air pollution is more complicated than city = bad, country = good. Air pollution, it turns out, is highly localized, so the back streets in a big city are significantly less polluted than busy streets in the same zip code. If there is a traffic jam, exposure to air pollutants varies depending on whether you're walking on one side of the road or the other. Location matters enough that small children closer to the height of car exhausts will inhale more toxins than adults who stand taller.

So, if you're not about to move to the country, you can still help yourself and your family by taking the back streets.

SEE ALSO
Wishcycling, *56*
An Idling Car, *142*

POLLUTION IS HIGHLY LOCALIZED

TAKE THE BACK STREETS

Moon pools are protected entrances to and from water that can even function when submerged. First created to support drilling operations on offshore platforms, they can include entrances on the decks or undersides of ships or an entry and exit for divers from permanent underwater research bases.

To enter the water from a submerged chamber below sea level, the trick is to pressurize the air around the pool to the same pressure as the surrounding water. The raised pressure keeps the water from gushing in and enables swimming pool-like access even though you're already below the surface.

SEE ALSO
The Overview Effect, *78*
Surfing Breaks, *212*

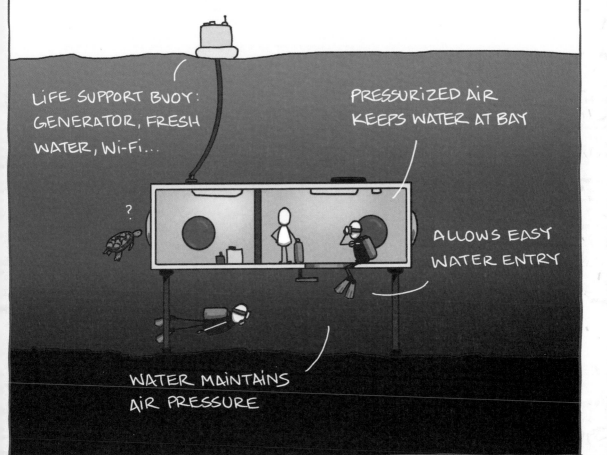

Pouring snacks into a hand rather than reaching into the bag (or bowl) keeps dirty hands and germs out of the snacks for others. I learned this from backpacking—no one wants to get sick two days into a four-day wilderness trip thanks to dirty hands—but it's beneficial in any context. It works in much the same way that a drinking fountain allows everyone to drink hygienically by bringing the water to your mouth rather than everyone's mouth to the water.

SEE ALSO
The Swiss Cheese Model, *10*
Dracula Sneeze, *196*

POUR, DON'T DIP WHEN SHARING SNACKS

TO MINIMIZE THE SPREAD OF GERMS

 INTRODUCES GERMS FROM HANDS TO THE BAG

 KEEPS GERMS OUT

PEOPLE OFTEN SAY THAT MOTIVATION DOESN'T LAST.

DAY 1

DAY 2

DAY 3

WELL NEITHER DOES BATHING —

DAY...

THAT'S WHY WE RECOMMEND IT DAILY.

—ZIG ZIGLAR

What should you take with you when you head out to the wilderness? Many items may prove handy, but a wise set to start from is the 10 Essentials.

The list is geared toward preparing for emergencies or an unexpected night in the wild. This version focuses on what the essential objects need to do rather than which objects you should bring. For example, insulation might be warm clothes but can sometimes be a windbreaker or good waterproofs for snow or rain. The 10 Essentials are just the basics—plan each trip thoughtfully and take care out there!

Rock climber Steve McClure wrote this handy limerick covering all 10 to help check that you have what you need.

To navigate, head for the sun
With first aid and knife on the run
Bring fire and shelter
Extra food is a helper
But water and clothes weigh a ton

SEE ALSO
Find The North Star, *100*
Pour, Don't Dip When Sharing Snacks, *150*
The Three-Day Effect, *230*

THE 10 ESSENTIALS

FOR WILDERNESS SAFETY

NAVIGATION

SUN PROTECTION

INSULATION

LIGHT

FIRST AID

FIRE

REPAIRS + TOOLS

NUTRITION

HYDRATION

SHELTER

Here's one of those happy occasions when we get our own win-win: The better we sleep, the better we can exercise, and the better we exercise, the better we sleep.

One of my more surprising reads was Novak Djokovic's *Serve to Win*, about diet, discipline, going gluten-free and physical and mental excellence. The legendary tennis pro certainly knows about excellence. Djokovic's parents ran a pizzeria, so he was especially dismayed to discover he had developed a gluten and lactose intolerance and a slight allergy to tomatoes. Learning about his philosophy on eating and taking care of yourself, including a deep respect for sleep, was illuminating. He highlighted this simple, virtuous cycle that many of us could benefit from. Since finishing the book, I created a nightly reminder to respect my sleep. Sleep well!

SEE ALSO
Taller in the Morning, *258*
Sleep Basics, *264*

THE VIRTUOUS CYCLE OF
EXERCISE AND SLEEP

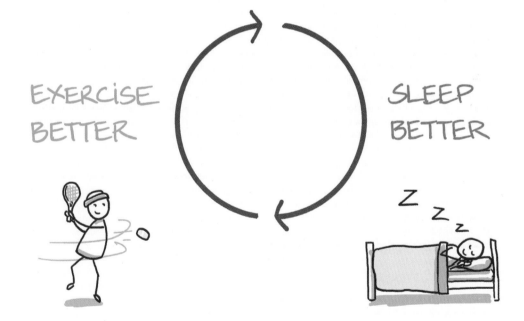

EXERCISE
BETTER

SLEEP
BETTER

You may have noticed that sometimes when the moon rises over the horizon, it seems unusually large. On several occasions, I've stopped to wonder at it shining behind the skyline—it's always a treat. However, if you stay awake long enough, you might see that later in the night, once the moon has risen higher in the sky, it has reverted to its expected size. This apparent change in size is known as the moon illusion.

Great minds from Aristotle to Isaac Newton have wondered at its cause, and I was surprised to learn that it's still debated. The most accepted explanations suggest the illusion arises from comparing the moon as it passes the horizon with known objects, such as buildings and trees, which provide a sense of scale. Higher in the sky, we can only compare the moon to the vastness of space and the sheer size of the sky itself. To experience the full grandeur, try a telephoto lens.

SEE ALSO
Atmospheric Perspective, *18*
Phases of the Moon, *176*

THE MOON ILLUSION

SEEMS SMALLER
WHEN UP IN THE SKY

SEEMS BIGGER
WHEN ON THE HORIZON

These signs of impending relationship doom take their names from the biblical end of days because, left unchecked, they can be an omen for the death of a once-healthy relationship. Psychologist John Gottman and his team, who identified the four horsemen of relationship apocalypse, can assess whether a couple displays the characteristics that lead to divorce by watching just minutes of a conflict conversation.

The four horsemen are:

Criticism: framing problems as the partner's defect
Defensiveness: counterattacking, whining, being the innocent victim
Contempt: talking down from a position of superiority, insults, eye-rolling, name-calling—the most dangerous of all
Stonewalling: withdrawing from the conflict, refusing to engage

Fortunately, the four horsemen have their antidotes, traits Gottman saw the masters of relationships using like complaining without blame, accepting responsibility, staying respectful and self-soothing.

SEE ALSO
Emotional Hot Potato, *236*

THE 4 HORSEMEN OF RELATIONSHIP APOCALYPSE

AND THEIR ANTIDOTES

CRITICISM

"You're so lazy!"

✓ Complain without blame. Use "I" instead of "you".

DEFENSIVENESS

"Ugh, We're late again." "How can I get ready if you're in the shower??"

✓ Accept responsibility for part of the conflict.

CONTEMPT

"What were you even thinking?!"

✓ Stay respectful. Appreciate small things often.

STONEWALLING

"Just forget it."

✓ Take time out to calm down and self-soothe.

This is not rocket science, but growing up, I tended to use the words kayak and canoe interchangeably out of ignorance. There are so many neat hybrid ways to get on the water now that nothing is as cut-and-dried as it once was. However, if you refer to the attributes in the sketch, you can be pretty confident you'll get your campsite watercraft right.

SEE ALSO
Flying Fabrics, *198*
Surfing Breaks, *212*

WHAT'S THE DIFFERENCE BETWEEN A

KAYAK AND CANOE

USUALLY OPENS IN THE CENTER (EXCEPT SIT-ONS)

SEATED WITH LEGS OUT IN FRONT

SEATED WITH LEGS TUCKED OR KNEELING

USUALLY OPEN FULL LENGTH

DOUBLE-BLADED PADDLE FOR ALTERNATE STROKES

SINGLE-BLADED PADDLE

Clouds come in an infinite variety, yet a few simple features—shape and height—will help you identify many of the most common types.

Stratus clouds—from the Latin meaning spread or laid out—are horizontal, featureless clouds that can cover the sky. They form when air rises slowly and may produce multiple layers.

In contrast to stratus clouds, cumulus clouds form when air rises more quickly. They are the puffy, fluffy, classic clouds that come to mind when you're asked to think of a cloud.

Cirrus clouds are the wispy curls like hair way up high.

Mid-level clouds use the prefix "alto-" and high-level clouds use "cirro-." So, for example, a mid-level cumulus cloud becomes altocumulus, and a high-level stratus cloud becomes cirrostratus.

SEE ALSO
Lake Effect Snow, *108*
Know Your Space Objects, *188*

KNOW YOUR CLOUDS

CLOUDS ARE MOSTLY ORGANIZED BY SHAPE AND HEIGHT.
COMBINE BOTH TO IDENTIFY

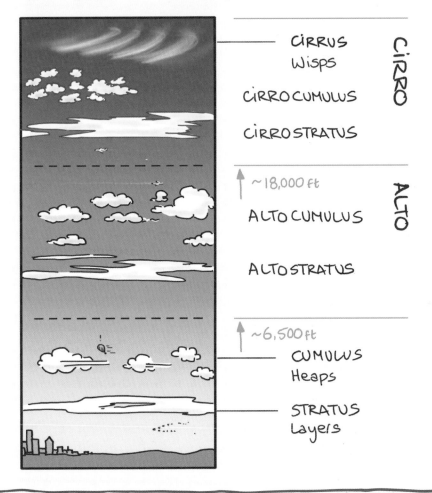

CIRRUS
Wisps

CIRROCUMULUS

CIRROSTRATUS

CIRRO

↑ ~18,000 ft

ALTOCUMULUS

ALTOSTRATUS

ALTO

↑ ~6,500 ft

CUMULUS
Heaps

STRATUS
Layers

This formula is a lovely start for most simple branding and can help in other areas of your life, whether you're a design professional or just seeking a few color combos for your home. Think of the example of a suit where about 60 percent of the color you see is the suit jacket and pants, 30 percent is the shirt and 10 percent is accent or highlight—the tie. Memorable and classic.

SEE ALSO
Let Your Data Speak for Itself, *52*
The Rule of Thirds, *94*

THE 60-30-10 COLOR RULE
FOR A SIMPLE AND EFFECTIVE COLOR SCHEME

LIKE FOR A SUIT...

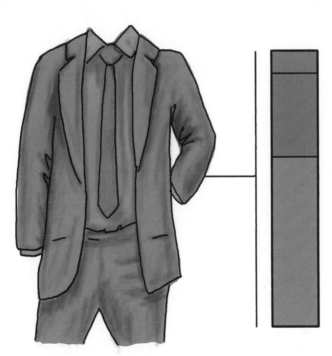

ACCENT
10% TIE

SUPPORTING
30% SHIRT

BASE
60% SUIT

The IKEA Effect is the increase in value we feel towards self-made products—products that required our effort to create them. Or, less formally, we love it more if we made it.

The effect is named after the odd sense of satisfaction many of us feel after spending more time and sweat than expected putting together IKEA's famous flat-pack creations. Yet not only does more effort equal more love, if we've put effort into something ourselves, we're also more likely to, often mistakenly, think that others will value it more, just as we do.

Duke University psychology professor and author, Dan Ariely, conducted several experiments leading to these conclusions. He also points out that kids are the ultimate expression of the IKEA effect: they're very hard, they don't come with instructions and they take a lot of effort.

SEE ALSO
Flow, *106*
The Benjamin Franklin Effect, *262*

THE IKEA EFFECT

WE LOVE IT MORE IF WE MADE IT

Ghost fishing is a sad reality of the fishing industry through which lost or discarded fishing gear continues to fish. It can be particularly troublesome as smaller trapped animals entice larger predators, who themselves get tangled. A net, after all, can continue to work whether people are around to pull it in or not. Recovering lost fishing gear is a challenging and often dangerous job, but organizations like Ghost Diving have made it their mission to remove dangerous debris.

SEE ALSO
Moon Pool, *148*
Countershading, *228*

GHOST FISHING
FISHING BY LOST OR ABANDONED FISHING GEAR

LOST FISHING GEAR
CONTINUES TO FISH

... ATTRACTING PREDATORS
WHO ARE CAUGHT IN TURN

...AND SO ON...

It can be hard to really believe the world's getting warmer if you're in a snowstorm or struggling to stay warm.

I like this simple analogy distinguishing between weather and climate from climate reporter Kendra Pierre-Louis: If weather is like the money in your pocket on any day, climate is like your net wealth over time. Climate, like wealth, generally changes slowly, but hopefully steadily, while any money in your pocket changes daily.

While there are many causes of extreme weather, this analogy helps keep some overall perspective even amid an unexpected cold snap.

SEE ALSO
The Overview Effect, *78*
Know Your Clouds, *164*

IF THE WORLD'S GETTING WARMER HOW COME IT CAN BE SO COLD OUT?

An analogy

WEATHER

is like

THE MONEY IN YOUR POCKET

on any one day

CLIMATE

is like

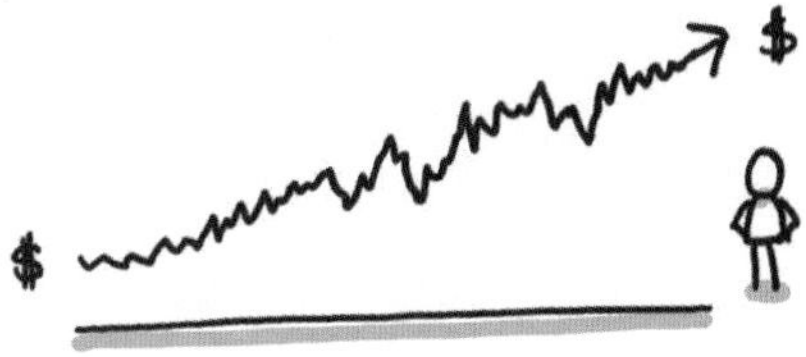

YOUR NET WEALTH

over time

Earth sits in the Goldilocks Zone: The range around a star that's not too hot or too cold to support liquid water. And liquid water is vital to sustaining life like we have on Earth.

If we lived too close to the sun, we'd roast. The average temperatures on Mercury and Venus are hot enough to boil water (and then some). And on Mars, the next planet farther out than Earth, the average temperature sits around -80 degrees F, cold enough to freeze water solid.

If you want to look for planets that might support life as we know it in distant star systems, looking for worlds occupying each star's Goldilocks Zone is a promising start.

SEE ALSO
Solar System Sizes, *12*
States of Matter, *96*

THE GOLDILOCKS ZONE
THE CIRCUMSTELLAR HABITABLE ZONE
JUST RIGHT TO SUPPORT LIQUID WATER

CONDITIONS FOR LIQUID WATER

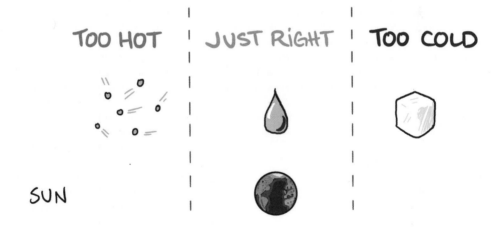

TOO HOT | JUST RIGHT | TOO COLD

SUN

Everyone is familiar with a crescent and full moon, but it's also good to know that a gibbous moon is when a crescent of shadow eats into the bright circle and that the hardest moon to see is a new one. When the lit area of the moon gets lighter day by day, the moon's in its waxing phase (growing), and when the moon darkens day by day, it's in the waning phase (shrinking). A handy rhyme to know whether the moon will get lighter or darker is "If it's light on the right, it's gonna get bright." Remarkably, we only ever see one side of the moon. To see the far side, you'd need to get in a spacecraft.

SEE ALSO
The Southern Cross, *102*
The Moon Illusion, *158*

PHASES OF THE MOON

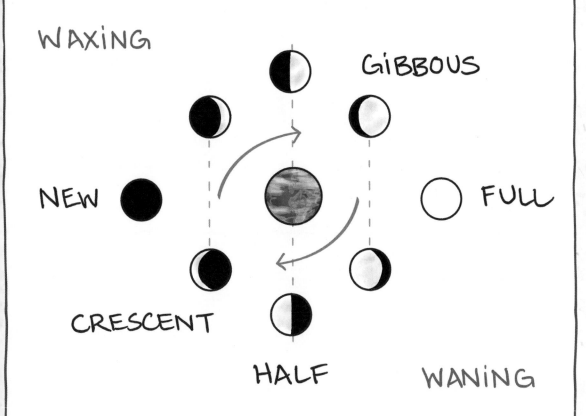

Tectonic plates are the giant pieces of the earth's crust that shift slowly under our feet. Where and how each plate meets another produces three primary types of plate boundaries. The plates either push together (convergent), slide away (divergent) or rub past each other (transform).

If you stand on the ground in an expansive landscape, it's striking to think just how remarkable an idea it is. The idea that the ground beneath our feet is moving with enough force to pull South America and Africa apart, or to thrust the Himalayas up from sea level was not obvious nor without contention. The acceptance of the fact, however, has given us a clearer understanding of our world.

SEE ALSO
Mercator Projection, *64*
Double-Landlocked Countries, *110*

TECTONIC PLATE BOUNDARIES

THE 3 MAIN TYPES

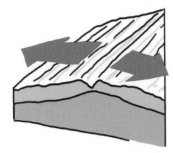

DIVERGENT

PLATES MOVING AWAY
FROM EACH OTHER
- Mid-Atlantic ridge
- The Great Rift Valley

CONVERGENT

PLATES COMING
TOGETHER
- The Andes
- The Himalayas

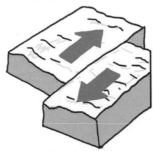

TRANSFORM

PLATES SLIDING PAST
EACH OTHER
- San Andreas Fault
- Dead Sea Transform

Two-factor authentication increases security by requiring two different types of proof of identity. So, rather than asking for two passwords, two-factor authentication might ask for a password along with your fingerprint, adding another failsafe against unwanted intrusion.

The usual factors involved ask for two of the following three things:
1. Something you know
2. Something you are
3. Something you have

Common examples of two-factor authentication include photo ID—you provide the ID card (something you have), and you must also look like the photo (something you are). Or a credit card (something you have) with a pin (something you know).

SEE ALSO
Types of Phishing, *40*
Decimal vs. Binary, *138*

2 FACTOR AUTHENTICATION
IDENTIFYING USING 2 OF THESE 3 FACTORS

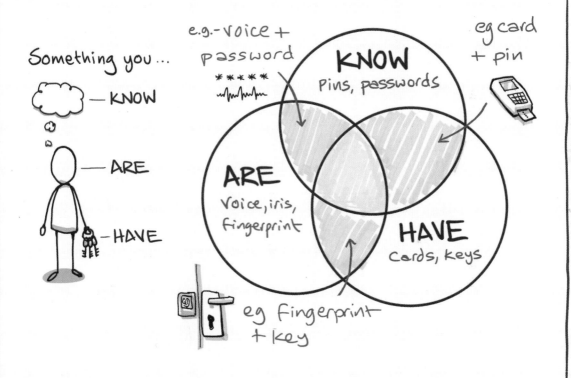

Something you...

— KNOW

— ARE

— HAVE

e.g.- voice + password
****

eg card + pin

KNOW
Pins, passwords

ARE
Voice, iris, fingerprint

HAVE
Cards, keys

eg fingerprint + key

I'VE MISSED MORE THAN 9,000 SHOTS
IN MY CAREER.

I'VE LOST ALMOST 300 GAMES.
26 TIMES I'VE BEEN TRUSTED
TO TAKE THE GAME-WINNING SHOT
AND MISSED.

I'VE FAILED OVER AND OVER AND OVER
AGAIN IN MY LIFE,
AND THAT IS WHY I SUCCEED.

— MICHAEL JORDAN

MoSCoW prioritization is a simple tool to help you decide what to do by sorting aspects of a project into Must Haves, Should Haves, Could Haves and Won't Haves. Developed for software delivery at Oracle by Dai Clegg, the technique helps overcome problems with simpler prioritization approaches—for example, sorting into high, medium or low—that rely on relative priorities without a clear definition of each.

When using this method, ideally, must-have activities would represent no more than 60 percent of the effort, so the confidence in delivering the project can remain high. But perhaps the most useful category is Won't Haves, as it manages expectations around what won't get done, at least not the first time around.

SEE ALSO
RACI, *60*
Yak Shaving, *242*

MoSCoW PRIORITIZATION

A WAY OF DECIDING WHAT TO DO NEXT

MUST	SHOULD	COULD	WON'T
MUST HAVE THESE TO WORK	IMPORTANT BUT CAN BE DONE LATER OR ANOTHER WAY	DESIRABLE BUT NOT NECESSARY	WON'T GET THIS TIME BUT WOULD LIKE

 DO FIRST!

While our bodies will generally make light work of repairing a cut in our skin or even healing a bone, some animals are able to go much further. Deer and moose antlers are grown and shed each year, and a moose may have antlers that span six feet across and weigh upward of 40 pounds.

An axolotl can regenerate entire limbs, and a lizard a whole tail. A flatworm can survive being cut in two, with the back half even regrowing a head and brain. In many cases, sea stars are also capable of regrowing a lost limb, but what's more astonishing is that in some species of sea star, a lost limb contains everything it needs to regenerate an entirely new body.

SEE ALSO
Misleading Animal Names, *34*
Sacred Animals, *256*

ANIMALS THAT REGENERATE

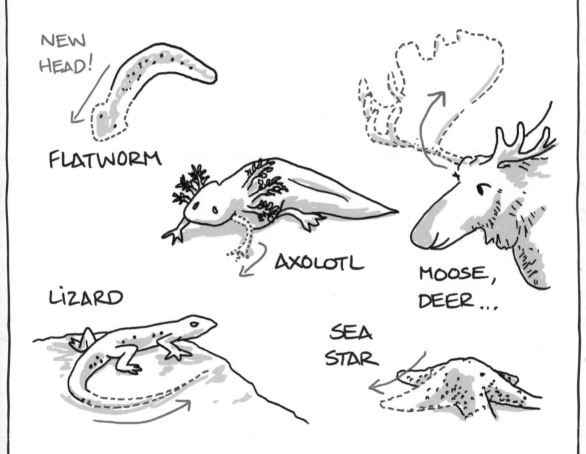

It's easy for space objects to blur into various rocky things flying around. This will help you tell them apart:

Comet: Comets are made of dust and ice. As comets approach the nearest part of their orbits to the sun, the dust and ice can vaporize, making them appear fuzzy and sending a long tail of debris into space.

Asteroid: Asteroids are big rocks orbiting the sun, mainly in the asteroid belt between Mars and Jupiter.

Meteor: A small piece of an asteroid or comet traveling through space, perhaps caused by a collision, is known as a meteoroid. Those that enter our atmosphere at high speeds are meteors and burn up with fiery trails. They're also known as shooting stars.

Meteorite: If the meteor makes it to the ground, it becomes a meteorite—a real piece of space you can touch.

SEE ALSO
Phases of the Moon, *176*
The Potato Radius, *214*

KNOW YOUR SPACE OBJECTS

COMET

FUZZY ORBITING OBJECT MADE OF ICE AND DUST WITH TAIL

ASTEROID

BIG ROCK ORBITING THE SUN

METEOR

ROCK BURNING UP THROUGH THE ATMOSPHERE

METEORITE

PARTS OF A METEOR THAT MADE IT ALL THE WAY TO THE GROUND

Proposed by computer scientist Bill Buxton, the Long Nose of Innovation helps us understand the process and impact of innovation. Buxton suggests that for any "wow" moment of new technology—the first mouse on the personal computer, touchscreens, haptics or self-driving cars—there has typically been a long period of low-amplitude invention, refinement and augmentation, often for 20 years or more. Technologies such as touchscreens need polishing, adjustment, optimization and often the development of an entire ecosystem to hit the big time.

One intriguing consequence of the theory is that the technologies that will have a substantial impact in the coming five years are likely 15 years old already. The next time you're wowed by a technology, consider the decades of small incremental improvements that were made before it reached you.

SEE ALSO
Thesis, Antithesis, Synthesis, *44*
Mohandas Gandhi's Path of Social Movements, *272*

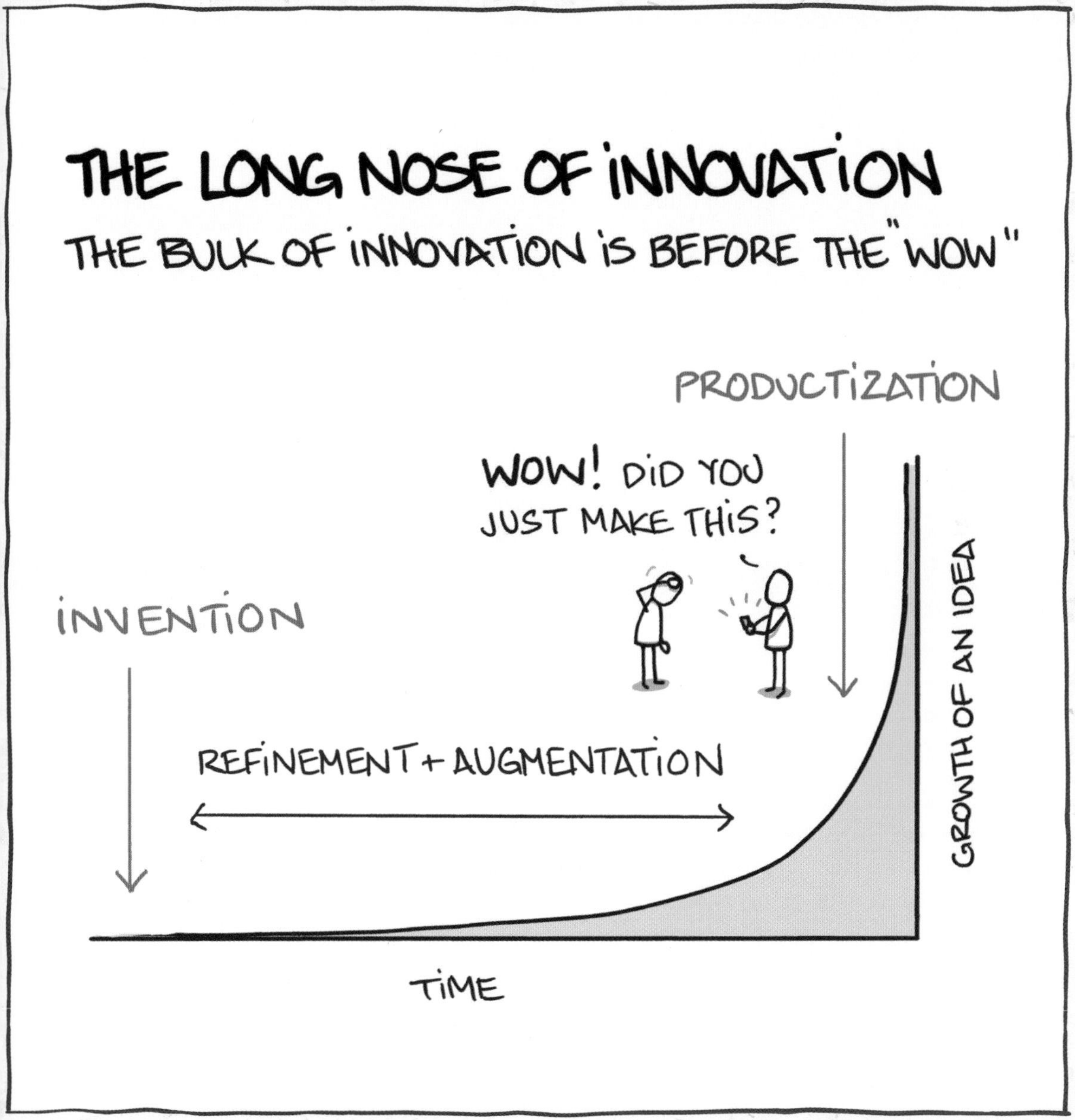
THE LONG NOSE OF INNOVATION
THE BULK OF INNOVATION IS BEFORE THE "WOW"
PRODUCTIZATION
WOW! DID YOU JUST MAKE THIS?
INVENTION
REFINEMENT + AUGMENTATION
GROWTH OF AN IDEA
TIME

Reliability is about getting the same results given the same conditions, and validity is measuring what you intend to measure. Understanding the difference can be harder than it sounds.

Suppose I want to measure how hardworking my children are, and I decided to time how long they spent on their homework. Within just a few days, it becomes apparent that the time varies based on the amount of homework. The children race quickly through some subjects while other subjects take longer, and one child finds his homework much easier than another child does without being any less hardworking.

Here, we have problems of validity—clearly, time spent on homework is not a valid measure by itself of how hard a child is working. And what's more, each time I retry the experiment, I might find the pattern to be different: problems of reliability.

This distinction shows up everywhere. Miscalibrated weighing scales will reliably read out the wrong weight every time, for example. But when it comes to people, establishing validity is often much harder. Does the best sports team always win the league? No. Why do they sometimes lose to the last-placed team? And do our school exams measure our actual intelligence and abilities or just how good we are at exams?

SEE ALSO
You Get What You Measure, *8*
The Spotlight Effect, *210*

UNDERSTANDING

RELIABILITY AND VALIDITY

THE SAME RESULTS IN THE SAME CONDITIONS	MEASURING WHAT YOU INTEND TO MEASURE

AIM IS OFF

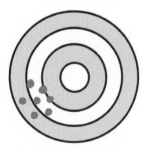

BUT PRETTY CONSISTENT

☑ RELIABLE
☐ VALID

AIM IS TRUE

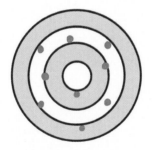

BUT DIFFERENT EVERY TIME

☐ RELIABLE
☑ VALID

AIM IS TRUE

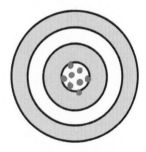

AND VERY CONSISTENT

☑ RELIABLE
☑ VALID

Sticky notes, spearheaded by the Post-it, have made their way into office folklore and remain a preferred choice for group collaboration, handy reminders and scribbled to-do lists. But the weak glue that makes them possible—paradoxically, they both stick and can be unstuck—means they are likely to end up on the floor after a few days attached to a board or monitor.

A common cause of notes falling sooner than intended is removing the sticky note from the stack by pulling diagonally. Once stuck on, this technique leads to a note peeling back from the top corner. And once it starts peeling, that note is coming down.

Instead, when removing the sticky note, keep your hand level and pull back forward and straight. This technique avoids a curling corner and will keep your sticky notes stuck for days longer.

SEE ALSO
Fix Wobbly Tables, *48*
MoSCoW Prioritization, *184*

HOW TO PEEL A STICKY NOTE

SO IT DOESN'T FALL DOWN

DON'T

DO

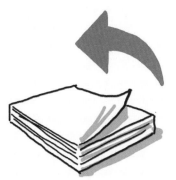

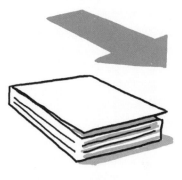

PEEL FROM
A CORNER

PULL FLAT
AND STRAIGHT

A Dracula sneeze is sneezing into your sleeve at your elbow rather than sneezing into your hands. The dramatic full Dracula pose is a fun reminder of a more hygienic way to sneeze should you be caught without a tissue. Keeping your hands clean by catching sneezes or coughs in this way helps reduce the chance of spreading cold and flu germs.

The Centers for Disease Control and Prevention's (CDC) preferred method for coughing and sneezing is to cover your mouth and nose with a tissue, throw it in the trash and wash your hands. But if you don't have a hanky handy, this method is much better than doing the deed directly into your hands or the air around you.

SEE ALSO
The Swiss Cheese Model, *10*
Pour, Don't Dip When Sharing Snacks, *150*

DRACULA SNEEZE

SNEEZING INTO YOUR SLEEVE HELPS PREVENT THE SPREAD OF COLD AND FLU GERMS

Parachuting, paragliding, hang gliding, kitesurfing, parasailing/parakiting and wingsuiting—all fun ways to get around and all very easy to mix up with each other. Paragliding is the closest I have ever felt to the joy of flying, even more so than when I once jumped out of a plane. Each form can be distinguished by a combination of how you launch, whether it has a rigid or flexible structure and whether you travel over water, land or through the air.

You might also look out for a paramotor—a big fan that's added to a paraglider—and winging, a cross between windsurfing and kitesurfing, where you hold directly onto a wing-shaped sail and let it whoosh you over the water.

SEE ALSO
Atmospheric Perspective, *18*
Kayak vs. Canoe, *162*

KNOW YOUR
FLYING FABRICS

PARACHUTE
Normally leaves from aircraft.
Designed to slow a fall.

WINGSUITING
Skydiving with a
webbed jumpsuit.

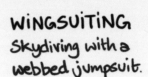

PARAGLIDER
Leaves from land.
No rigid structure.

HANG GLIDER
Leaves from land.
Rigid structure.

KITESURF
Pulls you along
over water.

PARASAIL/KITE
Lifted into the air.
Pulled by a boat.

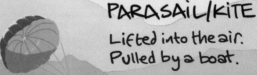

Alternatives researched, books bought and read, desk cleaned, no disruptions, sitting comfortably, inbox cleared, coffee in hand, ready to get started?

It's easy to be paralyzed by choices, unsure of our expertise, gnawed by doubt and uncertain if we're ready to give something a go. For many of us, the threshold is high to get started on the project in our heads, the plan to improve our finances or our new exercise regimen.

It's so easy to think we're not ready. Here's the actor Hugh Laurie with one of my favorite pieces of advice:

> *"It's a terrible thing, I think, in life to wait until you're ready. I have this feeling now that, actually, no one is ever ready to do anything. There is almost no such thing as ready. There is only now. And you may as well do it now. Generally speaking, now is as good a time as any."*

Getting started allows us to start learning. Sure, our first steps might be the wrong ones, but in starting, we soon find the right ones.

SEE ALSO
Find Your "Why Not?", *68*
The Role of a Finishing Line, *274*

BENEFITS TO SIMPLY GETTING STARTED

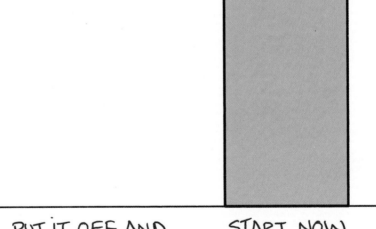

Perspective can be tricky to get your head around. In drawing and painting, using perspective creates the illusion of three-dimensional space on a flat surface. The simplest form to understand is one-point perspective. You will have experienced one-point perspective when looking down a corridor or the center of a street. If you extend the parallel lines of the walls and ground toward the center, they would appear to converge at a central point in front of you at eye level, known as the vanishing point. When real-life features are parallel like this, you can use a central vanishing point as a guide to help capture the scene accurately.

The simplicity of one-point perspective makes it impactful. Leonardo da Vinci, a personal hero of mine, famously employed one-point perspective in his mural *The Last Supper* in the Santa Maria delle Grazie convent in Milan. The vanishing point, carefully placed behind Jesus's head, draws the viewer's attention to the main subject of the scene.

SEE ALSO
Horizontal vs. Vertical Pupils, *252*

ONE-POINT PERSPECTIVE

We experience two-point perspective most clearly when we look at a large object, like a building, at an angle. With two-point perspective, you'll see the parallel lines on different sides of the buildings converge not to the center but to two vanishing points, one on either side. Two-point perspective is very common in architectural drawings because it's so evident when viewing buildings. The horizon is typically behind the building because we view it from eye level. If you were a worm or a bird, the horizon would be below or above the building, and you'd experience three-point perspective.

SEE ALSO
The Rule of Thirds, *94*

TWO-POINT PERSPECTIVE

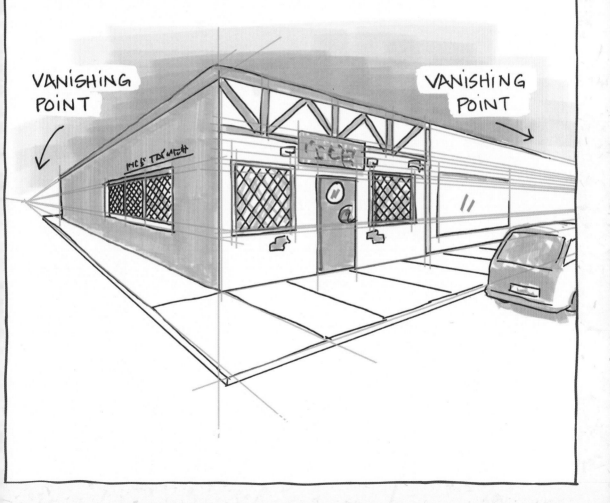

VANISHING POINT

VANISHING POINT

In three-point perspective, our vertical lines become angled, converging on a third vanishing point above or below. This contrasts with both one and two-point perspective where we draw our vertical lines vertical.

The simplest way to experience third-point perspective is to stand at the corner of a tall building like a church tower and look up. Not only will the sides of the church converge to vanishing points to either side, but the parallel vertical lines of the tower will appear to converge at some point high in the sky—our third vanishing point.

Three-point perspective makes for a more realistic scene, but it only becomes apparent when there's enough vertical relief, either up to the sky or below, in what we're viewing. As a result, we most commonly see it in views of downtown skyscrapers, perhaps with a caped or swinging superhero in the frame.

SEE ALSO
The Golden Ratio, *128*
The Square-Cube Law, *140*

THREE-POINT PERSPECTIVE

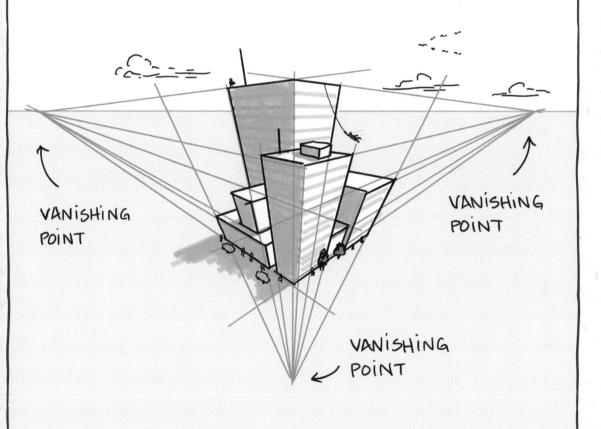

VANISHING POINT

VANISHING POINT

VANISHING POINT

INSIDE EVERY BLOCK OF MARBLE

DWELLS A BEAUTIFUL STATUE.

OFTEN ATTRIBUTED TO MICHELANGELO

The spotlight effect describes our tendency to overestimate how much attention people pay to our actions and appearance. While we may not be particularly proud of the skill we displayed in a game, a point that we made in a group discussion or a mistake we made on a project, evidence shows we are not good at gauging how much others are likely to notice compared to ourselves.

One memorable experiment had participants walk in late to a gathering wearing a conspicuous T-shirt with a large picture of Barry Manilow on the front. The T-shirt wearers later estimated how many others had noticed their T-shirt as significantly higher than what occurred in reality. Other studies looked at our assessment of how much others noticed positive or negative points we made in discussions with similar results.

I like the spotlight effect because it implies that we can all relax a little. It's human nature to consider what other people think of us. Yet, the truth is that other people are probably not thinking about us at all: They may very well be thinking about themselves.

SEE ALSO
The Awkwardness Vortex, *246*
The 20/40/60 Rule, *260*

While no two waves are identical, the shapes and features of the seabed and coastline combine to make three common types of surf break.

Beach breaks typically occur when waves form on the sandy build-up to a beach. They're great for beginners as the beach bottom can be more forgiving than coral or rock alternatives, and it's unlikely to be too far to paddle to.

Reef breaks form where a reef rises near the surface. This could be close to shore or quite far out, where the water can otherwise be deep. A reef's fixed and abrupt nature can create consistent waves, but a spiky, shallow reef can be painful for wipeouts.

Point breaks form around a headland or rocks jutting out from the coast. The waves usually extend into a bay on one or both sides of the projection and can provide some of the longest waves to surf.

SEE ALSO
Kayak vs. Canoe, *162*
Tectonic Plate Boundaries, *178*

SURFING BREAKS

THE 3 MAIN TYPES

BEACH BREAK

- OFTEN DON'T HAVE TO PADDLE FAR
- CAN CHANGE AS SAND SHIFTS
- WIPE OUTS MORE FORGIVING

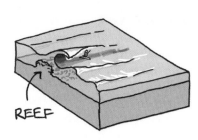

REEF

REEF BREAK

- CAN BE OUT AT SEA
- OFTEN FANTASTIC, CONSISTENT WAVES
- NASTY FOR WIPEOUTS

POINT

POINT BREAK

- FORMS AROUND A HEADLAND
- CAN BE LONG, CONSISTENT WAVES
- CAREFUL OF THE ROCKS!

When asked to picture an asteroid, most of us imagine a lumpy, bumpy rock, like a potato. So close is the resemblance in fact that some of the asteroid models in the film *The Empire Strikes Back* actually were potatoes. In contrast, thinking about a much larger rocky planet brings a smooth ball shape to mind. The potato radius is the size at which a space rock is more likely to be spherical rather than irregular like a potato.

For a space rock with a radius (half its width) of between 200 and 300 kilometers, the body's mass generates sufficient gravity to pull the rock toward the center—somewhat like taking a crumpled paper ball and squeezing from all sides. This gravitational pull is enough to start rounding the rock into a sphere. Therefore, beyond this size a space rock will be less of potato-shaped asteroid and more like the tidy globe we expect from planets.

SEE ALSO
The Square-Cube Law, *140*
Know Your Space Objects, *188*

THE POTATO RADIUS

WHEN GRAVITY STARTS TO MAKE ASTEROIDS SPHERES

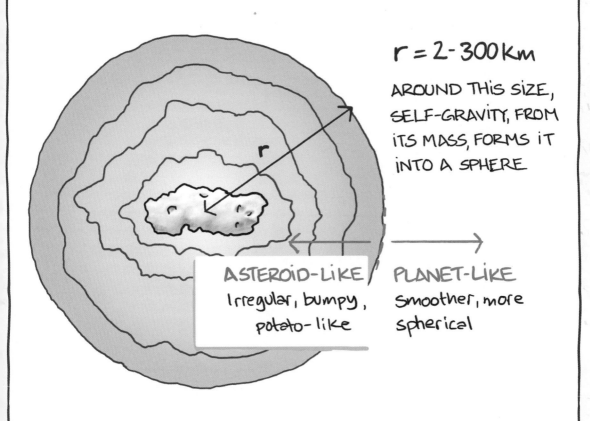

$r = 2-300\,km$

AROUND THIS SIZE, SELF-GRAVITY, FROM ITS MASS, FORMS IT INTO A SPHERE

ASTEROID-LIKE
Irregular, bumpy, potato-like

PLANET-LIKE
Smoother, more spherical

Have you ever noticed the pull of completing the last few pieces of a jigsaw puzzle? Or maybe it's the last clue of a murder mystery, the final chapter of a book or the ultimate mile of a marathon. Being close to our goal can motivate us to get to the end. That's the goal-gradient effect at work.

The goal-gradient effect may be part of why getting started is sometimes the most challenging part and may cause us to over-prioritize short-term goals to the detriment of later ones. In the example in the sketch, marketing professor Oleg Urminksy and coauthors found that as people approached the final stamp of a loyalty card toward a free coffee, they were more likely to buy coffee faster. And when issued with a new card, the rate of purchase dropped. The urgency diminished with the card blank and the perk once again distant.

The researchers also found that it wasn't the absolute distance from a goal but the perception of distance that mattered. People who started with a 12-stamp card with two stamps already completed tended to finish the card faster than those who started with an empty 10-stamp card, even though they were the same number of stamps from the goal. This related quirk of behavior is known as the endowed progress effect or the progress illusion.

SEE ALSO
The Paradox of Choice, *50*
Nine-Enders, *226*

THE GOAL-GRADIENT EFFECT

THE CLOSER WE GET TO A GOAL, THE HARDER WE TRY

CLOSER TO GOAL

FAR FROM GOAL

↑ MORE MOTIVATED   ↓ LESS MOTIVATED

The conscious competence learning model is handy to have in mind when you are learning or teaching a skill.

We are rarely competent at any new skill at first. If we continue working at it, we will eventually realize just how much we don't know. For example, having learned to swim when I was young, I always considered myself capable. Only much later, when taking a stroke technique class, did I realize how much I still had to learn. I've come to regard realizations such as these—a shift to conscious incompetence—as a happy achievement.

With effort, time and a good teacher, we may achieve conscious competence—performing the skill with conscious effort. Only later, after we have had sufficient practice for a skill to become automatic, can we achieve unconscious competence—effortlessly performing the skill without consciously thinking about it.

I learned that a final step takes you back to conscious competence. In this stage, you are not just excellent at the skill but also clearly aware of what you do that makes you excellent. This knowledge enables teaching the skill to others and is what, for example, helps make a great tennis player also become a great coach.

SEE ALSO
The OODA Loop, *124*
Johari Window, *132*

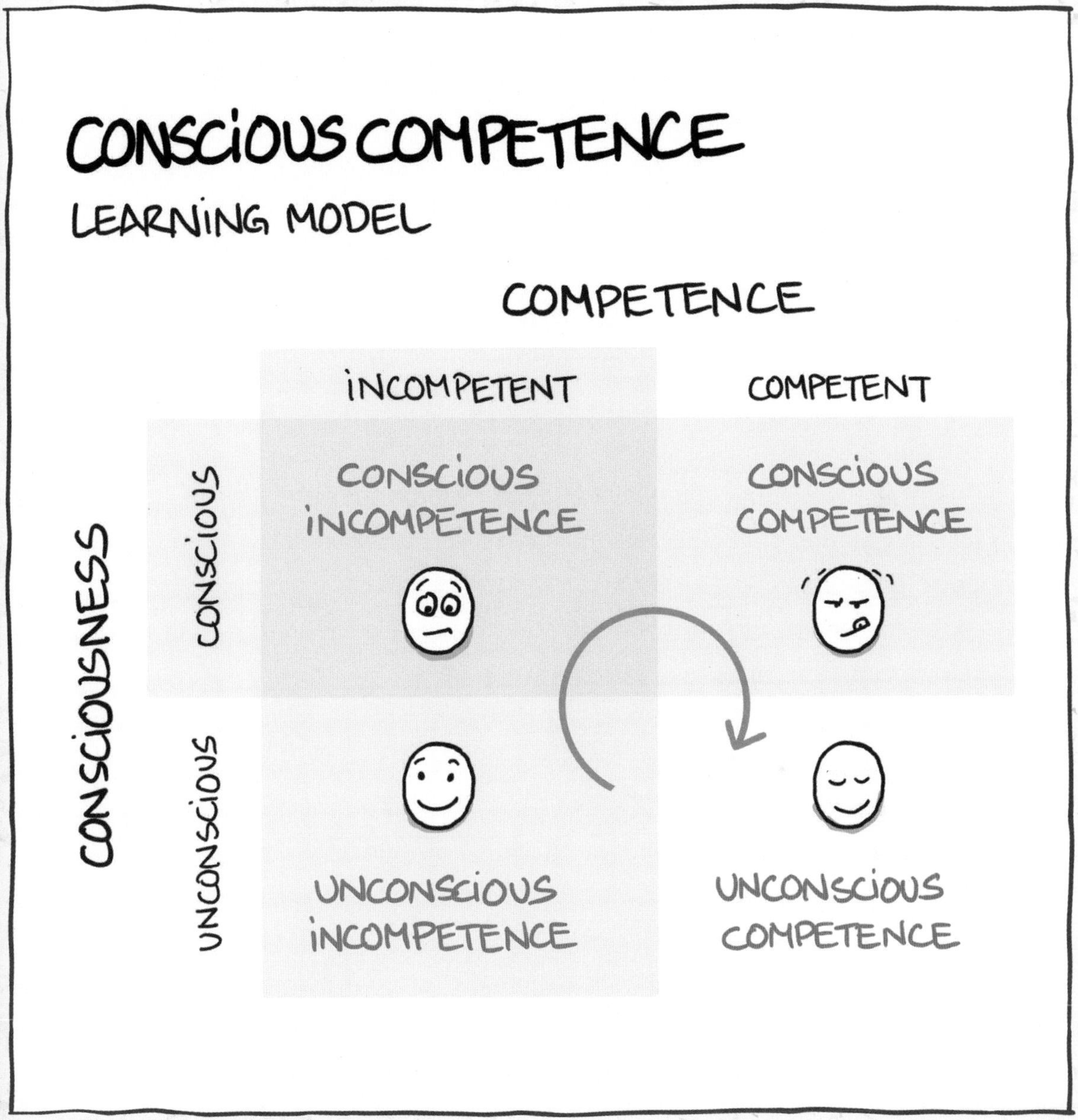

CONSCIOUS COMPETENCE
LEARNING MODEL

COMPETENCE

	INCOMPETENT	COMPETENT
CONSCIOUS	CONSCIOUS INCOMPETENCE	CONSCIOUS COMPETENCE
UNCONSCIOUS	UNCONSCIOUS INCOMPETENCE	UNCONSCIOUS COMPETENCE

CONSCIOUSNESS

Venomous animals inject venom through bites, stings and the like—think snakes, spiders, stingrays, wasps, etc. In contrast, poisoning is when a poison is passively transferred to us when we absorb, consume or inhale it—think amphibians, plants, fungi, etc. It might be through brushing up against some poison ivy, eating a poisonous animal or breathing in poisonous spores.

Only a few animals manage to be both venomous and poisonous, such as some snakes that inject venom and also have toxic skin from eating poisonous toads.

A third category you'll want to steer clear of is toxungenous animals that spray, fling or spit toxins toward potential threats. These include the skunk or the aptly named bombardier beetle, which sprays acid from its rear.

Fortunately, our instincts are well-trained from centuries of evolution and experience to help avoid anything venomous or poisonous, but one day you may find it pays to know the difference.

SEE ALSO
Misleading Animal Names, *34*
Sacred Animals, *256*

WHAT'S THE DIFFERENCE BETWEEN
VENOMOUS AND POISONOUS

VENOM INJECTED
THROUGH BITES,
STINGS&& THE LIKE

Snakes, spiders,
stingrays...

POISON ABSORBED
CONSUMED OR
INHALED

Amphibians, plants,
Fungi...

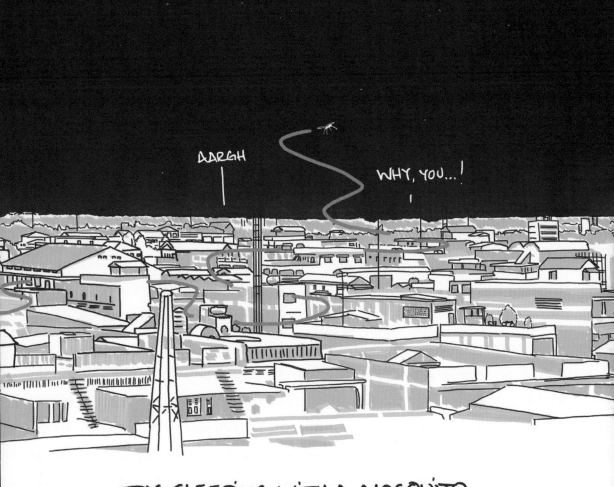

TRY SLEEPING WITH A MOSQUITO.

— AFRICAN PROVERB

We know it intuitively: Some people we know we can count on, while we feel the need to keep an eye on others. The trust battery is a metaphor that helps us visualize these trust levels.

This concept is from Shopify CEO Tobi Lütke. He suggests that in each interaction, we subconsciously consider the level of our trust battery. That level affects how we respond to people. The trust battery is a great tool to discuss trust in performance reviews without things getting too personal.

He explains, for example, that when a new colleague joins your company, the trust battery between the two of you may start at around half full. Each time the new colleague acts in a way that earns your trust, that level increases. And if they let you down, the level decreases. But watch out—while the trust battery fills up slowly over many interactions, it can quickly drain.

SEE ALSO
The Johari Window, *132*
The Trust Equation, *144*

TRUST BATTERY
THE LEVEL OF TRUST WE'VE BUILT FOR SOMEONE

I'M SURE ANA WILL DO IT, BUT FRED KEEPS FINDING EXCUSES

EACH INTERACTION

FILLS OR DEPLETES

Nine-enders are people in the last year of a decade, for example, those at age 29, 39, 49 or 59. In these nine-ender years, we're more likely to do something extreme and significant, like running a marathon for the first time. What's going on?

Social psychologists Adam Alter and Hal Hershfield, who coined the term nine-ender, propose that as we approach the end of a decade, we are more likely to do a meaningful audit of our lives. As we take stock of our goals or accomplishments, if we feel we've fallen short or if there's something else we want to accomplish, we're much more likely to do it during this period than in any other year of the decade. This increase in self-reflection and search for existential meaning means nine-enders are more likely to be training their hardest and sweating over a marathon finish line. So while turning 28 may have felt like turning 27 or 26, it may be very different from turning 29.

SEE ALSO
The Overview Effect, *78*
The Role of a Finishing Line, *274*

Countershading is a natural and disarmingly simple form of camouflage often found on dolphins, porpoises, whales, fish and birds. In the jungle or grasslands, perhaps stripes, spots or mottled colors help you fit in, but how do you hide against the uniform backdrop of the sea or sky?

An animal with countershading has a darker color on its back and top (the dorsal side) and a lighter color underneath (the ventral side). This simple strategy enables a dolphin, for example, to look light like the sky to animals watching from below while looking dark like the depths of the ocean to any creature above.

SEE ALSO
Moon Pool, *148*
Venomous vs. Poisonous, *220*

COUNTERSHADING
SIMPLE, NIFTY CAMOUFLAGE

DARK ON THE
DORSAL SIDE

LIGHT ON THE
VENTRAL SIDE

FROM
ABOVE

FROM
BELOW

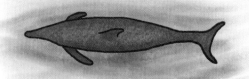

Something about being out in nature for three days or more resets us and improves our mood, well-being and mental acuity.

River rafting guide Ken Sanders noted the three-day effect after seeing a marked change in the groups he led on the third day of a river journey. By the third day, the river becomes like a new reality for the travelers, and their old reality fades away, Sanders explains. Since that original observation, cognitive neuroscientist David Strayer has conducted studies that measured an increase in participants' creativity and problem-solving after three or more days in nature. We start to think more clearly.

As we spend more time on our phones, laptops and devices, it's easy to spend less time in the great outdoors. Perhaps it's time to schedule a trip and turn our devices off. The three-day effect shows that the benefits we are missing out on may be significant.

As Sanders says, "I think it takes the first two days and nights to wash away whatever veneer of civilization you have brought with you. The new reality begins on that third day."

SEE ALSO
Solvitur Ambulando, 92
Notice When You're Happy, *104*

THE 3-DAY EFFECT

3 DAYS IN NATURE GIVES A POWERFUL RESET

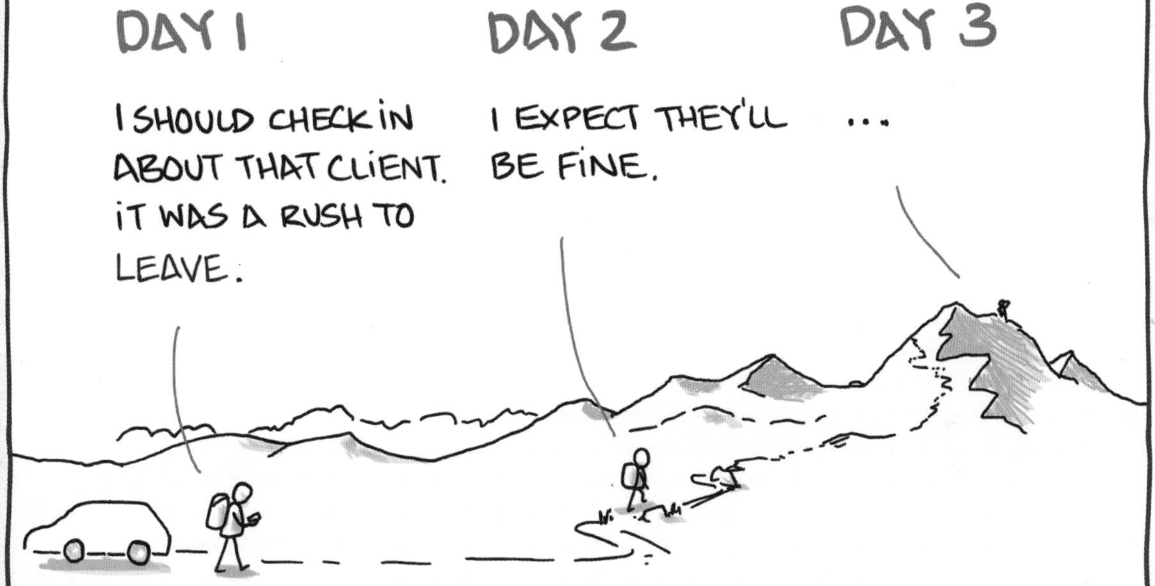

As a maxim, Chesterton's Fence is a caution to not take a fence down unless you understand why someone put it up.

The idea, named after English writer G.K. Chesterton, goes beyond property boundaries and borders. In a spirit of progress, it is tempting to want to do away with old designs, laws, policies or institutions that no longer seem to help. It's tempting to think that the people who made them weren't as bright as we are or that they didn't see things correctly.

Yet regulations, policies or fences are not usually built by accident— they required effort and action. Before we uproot an idea that seems outdated, old or useless, Chesterton's Fence reminds us that if a fence exists, there was likely a reason. Take the example of a workplace safety precaution that starts to be ignored: it was likely the response to a worksite accident, or even death. It may well be that change is needed, but considering why the fence is there in the first place is often a good starting point for dialogue about whether or not we still need it or can improve upon it.

SEE ALSO
The Law of Unintended Consequences, *114*
Mohandas Gandhi's Path of Social Movements, *272*

The Diderot effect describes how a new purchase can lead to a spiral of replacing existing possessions that no longer live up to the new standard. The phenomenon is named after 18th-century French philosopher Denis Diderot, who wrote the entertaining and unusually titled essay "Regrets on Parting with My Old Dressing Gown." In it, Diderot describes how his possessions no longer seemed up to scratch after he was given a flashy new scarlet dressing gown. Seeing this, he replaces his old straw chair with a leather one, a plank bookshelf with an inlaid armoire, a clay statue with a bronze statue and so on, emptying his savings. Whereas he was the master of his old dressing gown, he becomes a servant to the new one, guarding it from spills or burns.

More generally, the effect also highlights that we surround ourselves with objects that fit our sense of identity. On receiving something that reflects a new, aspirational identity, rather than rejecting the new thing, we may find ourselves replacing our old objects and selves to fit the new.

SEE ALSO
The IKEA Effect, *168*

THE DIDEROT EFFECT

ONE PURCHASE BEGETS ANOTHER

The boss yells at the employee, the employee yells at their spouse, the spouse yells at their child, the child yells at their younger sibling, the sibling yells at the dog, the dog pees on the rug. This scene is an excellent example of "emotional hot potato"—from Lawrence Cohen's book *Playful Parenting*—where the hot potato emotion makes its painful way through each family member.

Bad moods can be contagious, as can anger and anxiety. Our innate empathy can naturally transfer a bad mood from a coworker to ourselves. Emotional hot potato can also be a form of projection where we attempt to rid ourselves of an unpleasant emotion by transferring it or attributing it to others. By handling the hot potato of the anger of a teenage child, for example, the parent may find themselves seething while the child feels better having passed on the potato. To help break the cycle of negative emotions we might try playfully interrupting to defuse the tension, or not accepting the hot potato and asking instead, "what do you think you'll do?"

SEE ALSO
The Virtuous Cycle of Exercise and Sleep, *156*
The Awkwardness Vortex, *246*

EMOTIONAL HOT POTATO

SPREADING A BAD MOOD

Tsundoku is a beautiful Japanese word for the acquiring and piling up of books without reading them. It's constructed from two words that mean "piling up" (tsunde-oku) and "reading" (dokusho).

It's easy to fall prey to tsundoku. Immediately upon entering a bookstore, I'm filled with the promise of knowledge and entertainment that exudes from the books. Each book calls out to share its wisdom and the draw of quiet hours spent taking it in. And given it takes hours to read most books and only moments to buy them, practicing tsundoku is a common pastime.

The sketch is loosely based on my parents' bedroom growing up. They are experienced and talented "tsundokists."

SEE ALSO
Lifetime Reads, *80*
Sleep Basics, *264*

TSUNDOKU

THE ACT OF ACQUIRING BOOKS
AND LETTING THEM PILE UP
WITHOUT READING THEM

積ん読

Physics envy refers to the wish that your area of study were as precise, predictable, repeatable and amenable to modeling and replication as physics is.

As it turns out, most fields that involve people—such as economics and the social sciences—are rarely as tidy, orderly and neatly mathematically modeled as physics. Instead, they are messy, uncertain and filled with context, nuance, history and other confounding factors.

And while we do our best to quantify and identify effects or cleanly isolate our cognitive biases or our quirks of behavioral psychology, rarely are they able to live up to the standards of physics. It's enough to turn one green with envy.

Physics envy reminded me of the best-laid plans of our Saturday sports coaches turning for their substitutes to execute their strategies, only to find the players climbing trees in the adjacent field.

SEE ALSO
The Law of Unintended Consequences, *114*
The BS Asymmetry Principle, *134*

PHYSICS ENVY

WISHING YOUR FIELD WAS PRECISE AND PREDICTABLE

Yak shaving is the concept that when you set out to do something, you find you have to do something else first, which requires you to finish this other thing, and so on until you find yourself shaving a yak, or doing an equally unrelated activity, in order to do the initial thing you set out to do.

It's pretty common in life (e.g., cleaning your room) and particularly resonates in coding where, when tackling one thing, you frequently find yourself fixing something else, which requires you to fix something else, and so on.

SEE ALSO
Idempotence, *112*
The Diderot Effect, *234*

YAK SHAVING

"DOING 'Z' TO DO 'Y' TO DO 'X'... SO YOU CAN DO 'A'"

DON'T ASK THE BARBER

IF YOU NEED A HAIRCUT.

In her book *Cringeworthy*, Melissa Dahl explores what makes an awkward moment feel awkward. She shares a cycle that many of us may relate to, perhaps in a job interview, when giving a talk or when telling a joke that falls flat.

It starts with feeling nervous: The body's reactions include butterflies in the stomach, raised heart rate, sweaty palms—you know the signals. As we notice these physical reactions, our attention turns inward and we become self-conscious. We may start worrying about our appearance, that there's no natural position for our arms or that our voice sounds funny. This makes us more nervous, and into the awkwardness vortex we go.

Fortunately, Dahl suggests several ways to break the cycle. Anxiety shares a lot of the same body signals as excitement, so reframing anxiety as excitement helps us trick ourselves into a more positive mindset and take our attention away from ourselves. And to break our self-consciousness, we can focus on anything outside of ourselves. Good luck!

SEE ALSO
The Spotlight Effect, *210*
The Conscious Competence Learning Model, *218*

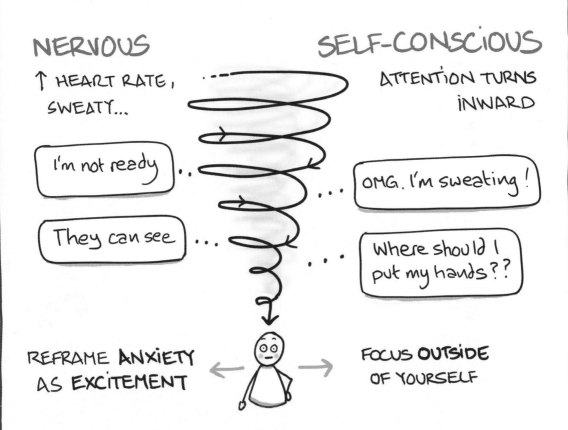

THERE'S NOTHING ABOUT
A CATERPILLAR

THAT TELLS YOU
iT'S GOING TO BE
A BUTTERFLY.

— BUCKMINSTER FULLER

Have you ever noticed that many stories follow a similar arc? While Kurt Vonnegut is best known for his imaginative stories, his self-proclaimed "prettiest contribution" to culture is a theory on the shapes of stories, presented in his rejected master's thesis.

The shapes describe varying trials of the main characters throughout a story on an axis of fortune—good fortune, wealth and good health at the top; ill fortune, sickness, poverty and trouble at the bottom. He illustrates, for example, the enduring popularity of what he calls the Man in Hole story, where a person in an above-average situation faces adversity and then regains their former position. Another example is the Boy Meets Girl story, in which an ordinary person experiences a turn for the better only to lose it and, after struggle and difficulty, get it back again to live happily ever after.

Vonnegut observes, however, that a trait of true literary masterpieces is that they often show how it's hard to tell whether something is really a turn for the better or worse.

SEE ALSO
Ordering Adjectives, *84*
Tsundoku, *238*

SHAPES OF STORIES
KURT VONNEGUT'S TIMELESS ANALYSIS

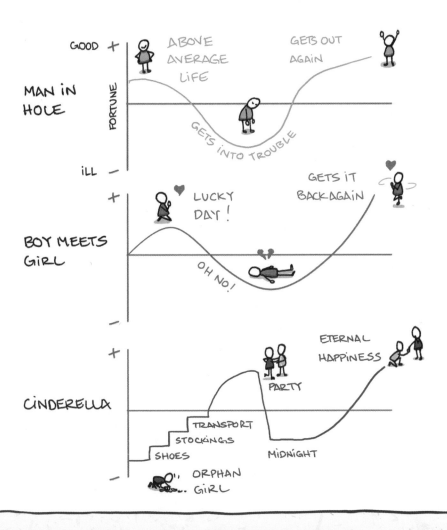

Look deeply into your neighbor's eyes and you'll see two round pupils. But look at a crocodile or snake's eyes— from a distance, of course—and you'll see a fascinating, slightly sinister vertical slit-shaped pupil that your cat also shares. Meanwhile, goats and sheep have horizontal, largely rectangular pupils. What's going on?

Horizontal pupils tend to be shared by grazing herbivores: When positioned on the sides of a head, horizontal pupils create a sharp panoramic view. This feature is ideal for spotting predators in open terrain and while running, which is likely why they tend to belong to prey animals—they are optimized for fleeing.

Vertical pupils bring vertical contours into sharp focus while blurring horizontal ones. This feature makes them handy for estimating the ambush distance of prey. And slit pupils are generally more effective at adjusting how much light they let in than round ones. A human's round pupil can change in area by about 15 times to let in more or less light. In contrast, the slit pupil of a cat can change in area about 135 times. This adjustment makes the vertical slit perfect for ambush predators exploring by night.

Our round pupils, by contrast, are generalist's eyes. With the muscles for expanding and contracting uniformly arranged around the circular pupil, we benefit from an even focus across our view.

SEE ALSO
Misleading Animal Names, *34*
Sacred Animals, *256*

HORIZONTAL vs. VERTICAL
PUPILS   PUPILS

Sheep, goats, deer   cats, snakes, crocs

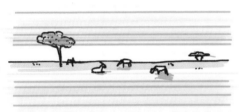 

Good for
WIDE FIELD OF VIEW   Good for
GAUGING PREY DISTANCE

Common among   Common among

↑ HERBIVORES   ↑ AMBUSH HUNTERS

↑ ACTIVE BY DAY   ↑ ACTIVE BY NIGHT

There's something innately enjoyable about throwing rocks into the sea, a lake, a river or even a large puddle. Even the smallest child gets a kick out of lobbing things into the water. Maybe it's the physicality of the motions, the satisfying sounds, the inexhaustible nature of it or the endless variation of the waves. In my experience, it's not long before rock throwing turns into rock skipping or skimming. Aiming for the most skips is as satisfying as it is elusive. So what's the perfect technique?

Ex-NASA engineer Mark Rober wanted to find out, so he repurposed a clay target launcher and adjusted each variable to find the perfect combination. Here's what worked best.

1. Throw at a 20-degree angle: Starting higher than you might think creates more potential energy for more bounces.

2. Spin fast: When spinning fast, the stone resists flipping over, so give your wrist a good flick.

3. Angle the rock at 20 degrees: While Step 1 is the angle at which the rock hits the water, this tip is about the angle of the rock itself. A stone tilted at this angle as it hits the water creates a perfect exit ramp to shoot back up and out.

4. Go flat and heavy: A smooth bottom matters more than shape or diameter, and a weightier rock has more momentum to keep on skipping.

Humans have coexisted with and relied upon animals throughout our time on the planet. They sustain us, protect us and sometimes prey on us, leading to many forms of animal worship (and sacrifice) across cultures.

Cattle, for example, are sacred in Hinduism and ancient Greek and Egyptian religions. The ancient Egyptians counted many animals among their gods, often with mixed human-animal forms with human bodies and animal heads, including Sekhmet the lion, Khnum the ram, Anubis the jackal, Nekhbet the vulture and Horus the falcon.

The Mayans worshiped many animals, one of the most sacred being the jaguar. It appears in many forms in their temples, including the dancing jaguar from Honduras shown in the sketch.

Animals play a central role in many tales from Native American cultures of the Pacific Northwest in the U.S., including Raven, known as the Trickster. Then there's the World Turtle from a Hindu legend where the world is carried on the back of four elephants standing on a turtle.

Some animals are even used to predict or divine the future, including Punxsutawney Phil, a celebrity groundhog who famously predicts the coming weather in Pennsylvania.

SEE ALSO
Hope, *70*
The Overview Effect, *78*

CARRIES
THE WORLD

THE WORLD
TURTLE

MAYAN, HONDURAS

JAGUAR

KNUM, ANCIENT
EGYPT

SOME
SACRED
ANIMALS

RAM

HINDU
+ MORE

SACRED COW

PACIFIC NORTHWEST
TRICKSTER

RAVEN

PUNXSUTAWNEY PHIL
!

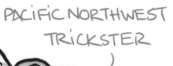

GROUNDHOG

Your height could be up to one centimeter more in the morning than at the end of the day thanks to the effect of gravity on your body.

Our spines are made up of vertebrae, and sandwiched between them are 23 spinal discs. The discs provide cushioning and flexibility and help keep the spine together, among other things. During the day, gravity slightly compresses the discs—as well as our joints. While we sleep, we are lying down and gravity no longer compresses the discs vertically, so the discs reabsorb fluid and nutrients to recover their original height.

Gravity's effect on our bodies is enough to create "space height." This is the height we reach after spending time in space, primarily due to the spine getting longer. NASA astronaut Kate Rubins left Earth at 5'7" tall and returned at over 5'8". Our height returns to normal weeks after returning to Earth.

SEE ALSO
The Virtuous Cycle of Exercise and Sleep, *156*
Sleep Basics, *264*

TALLER IN THE MORNING

WE SHRINK THROUGH THE DAY

1 OUR SPINES HAVE 23 POROUS DISCS BETWEEN OUR VERTEBRAE

2 DURING THE DAY, GRAVITY COMPRESSES EACH DISC AND SOME JOINTS A SMALL AMOUNT

3 WHILE WE SLEEP AT NIGHT, THEY REABSORB LIQUID TO RECOVER FULL HEIGHT

It's an old maxim. At age 20, we worry about what others are thinking of us. When we reach 40, we decide we don't care what others think of us. And then, when we're 60, we discover that all this time, no one was thinking about us at all.

The 20/40/60 rule has several facets. On the one hand, the implication that no one thinks about you can be disheartening, unless you make it empowering. About to tackle something hard? Don't expect others to be cheering or thinking about it as much as you are. See something that needs to improve? It's up to you to make that change. On the other hand, there is the uplifting message that we don't need to worry as much about our mistakes. We each have our own stuff to think about. Others are likely too busy worrying about their mistakes to worry about yours.

SEE ALSO
The Spotlight Effect, *210*

THE 20/40/60 RULE

At age
20
WE WORRY
WHAT OTHERS
THINK OF US

At age
40
WE DON'T CARE
WHAT THEY
THINK OF US

At age
60
WE DISCOVER
THEY WEREN'T
THINKING OF US

In his autobiography, Benjamin Franklin relates how he needed to win over a man who opposed his position as clerk of the General Assembly. He chose to use an old maxim: "He that has once done you a kindness will be more ready to do you another, than he whom you yourself have obliged." To do this, he asked to borrow a "very scarce and curious book" from his opposition, which he returned with a note of thanks. When they next met, the man spoke to him "with great civility," and they even became friends until his death.

It's a strange and counterintuitive approach. Naturally, many of us assume we would be inclined to like those who help us. Yet here we have the opposite. Explanations of the effect lean on our self-perception and consistency. Despite what we tend to think, sometimes it's our actions that drive our beliefs rather than our beliefs that drive our actions. As the saying goes, "It's easier to act yourself into a new way of thinking than think yourself into a new way of acting."

When the man finds himself helping Franklin, he tries to explain his own behavior, and his logic suggests he wouldn't have helped him if he didn't like him. Therefore, he must like him.

SEE ALSO
The Ikea Effect, *168*
The 20/40/60 Rule, *260*

THE BENJAMIN FRANKLIN EFFECT
WE'RE INCLINED TO LIKE PEOPLE WE HELP

I HELPED THEM > I HELP PEOPLE I LIKE > I LIKE THEM...?

ACTION   EXPLANATION   BELIEF

Sleep is a wonderful thing—the state in which we grow, repair our bodies, process our thoughts, refresh our minds and bodies and recharge. But sleep is not just one thing. Researchers have identified different stages and types of sleep that we pass through on a typical night.

Sleep includes both REM (Rapid Eye Movement) sleep and non-REM sleep. REM sleep is when we do our most vivid and emotion-filled dreaming and, as you might imagine, is accompanied by rapid movements of the eyes. Non-REM sleep has several stages, from light sleep in stages one and two, when we're almost awake, to the deeper stages three and four.

Typically REM and non-REM sleep alternate every 90 to 110 minutes. We have more non-REM sleep earlier, including most of our deepest sleep. In later sleep cycles, REM sleep will make up more of our sleep time. This distribution of REM sleep means that if you cut your sleep short by a couple of hours, you can miss a significant proportion of your REM sleep.

We spend 36 percent of our lives asleep, meaning if you live until you're 90, you'll have slept for around 32 years!

SEE ALSO
The Virtuous Cycle of Exercise and Sleep, *156*
Taller in the Morning, *258*

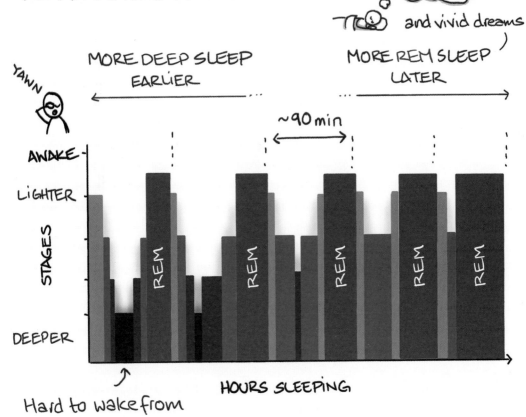

We expect the pace of life in the big city to be faster than in a small town. It turns out this is true in a more literal sense than one might imagine. In his book *Scale*, physicist Geoffrey West shares data from researchers who measured walking speeds in various cities and found that the larger the city, the faster people walked.

Walking pace is the result of several factors. Our social interactions, lifestyles, what's happening around us and how others behave all affect how quickly we feel the need to travel between one place and the next. These factors contribute to the fact that the walking speed of residents roughly doubles between small towns of a few thousand and cities of over a million people.

I didn't see data on it, but you might expect that there's a limit to how fast we're willing to walk/jog/run down the street, regardless of how big a city eventually gets. Taxi!

SEE ALSO
A World of Four Income Levels, *122*
1.5 Billion Heartbeats, *130*

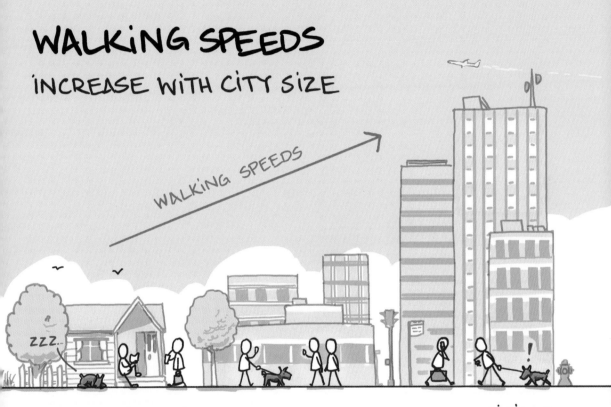

You might think adding more of a good thing would make the overall outcome better. And, yes, this natural intuition is often true, up to a point. However, the law of diminishing returns suggests that as you add more of a single factor, you are likely to yield progressively lower benefits.

It's like the old adage "Too many cooks spoil the broth." Another cook or two might help, but beyond that, they'll probably start getting in each other's way. Aside from cooking broth, you might see the law play out in other areas of life such as studying for exams, how money affects your happiness, or the number of people working on a project at work.

SEE ALSO
MoSCoW Prioritization, 184
The Long Nose of Innovation, *190*

Live sporting events have been a staple of the human experience for thousands of years. These days, millions of people worldwide turn out weekly to watch their teams compete against others in all types of sports. No doubt it must fill us with happiness and enjoyment, right? Well, it's not so clear-cut.

To find out how watching sports teams play affects our happiness, researchers at the University of Sussex used an app that pinged people randomly during the day and asked how they felt. They used this data to investigate how happiness changes in the build-up to a soccer match, during the match and in the hours afterward. They also looked at whether people's teams won or lost. They found that winning made people happy but not nearly as unhappy as losing made them.

If you attend a game and your team loses, especially if it was expected to win, the depth of your unhappiness is around double the happiness boost of winning—the pain felt was second only to being sick in bed. What's more, the pain of a loss lasts twice as long as the joy of a win. It's the supporters' paradox. If, on average, watching soccer makes people unhappy, why does it remain so popular? Perhaps because the joy of winning, according to the same study, is second only to lovemaking or intimacy with a partner.

SEE ALSO
Hope, *70*
Notice When You're Happy, *104*

THE SUPPORTERS' PARADOX

LOSING MAKES US
MORE UNHAPPY

...THAN WINNING
MAKES US HAPPY

SIGH

YES!

0 - 2

Mohandas K. "Mahatma" Gandhi is famous for leading the successful non-violent protests that led to India's independence from the British Empire. In the March 9, 1921, edition of *Young India*, he wrote that "Every good movement passes through five stages, indifference, ridicule, abuse, repression, and respect." His ideas have come to be known more colloquially by the phrase: First they ignore you, then they laugh at you, then they fight you, then you win.

This same pattern parallels the stages of grief, the adoption of innovations and the acceptance of new scientific ideas. For an alternative framing, Scottish geologist Charles Lyell quoted a popular saying attributed to Swiss-born American naturalist Louis Agassiz: "Whenever a new and startling fact is brought to light in science, people first say, 'it is not true,' then that 'it is contrary to religion,' and lastly, 'that everybody knew it before.'"

SEE ALSO
The BS Asymmetry Principle, *134*
The Long Nose of Innovation, *190*

MOHANDAS GANDHi'S
PATH OF SOCiAL MOVEMENTS

FIRST THEY
IGNORE YOU

THEN THEY
LAUGH AT YOU

THEN THEY
FIGHT YOU

THEN YOU
WIN

*"**Just remember that finishing lines are good, but their most important role is to get you over the start line in the first place.**"*

This wisdom is from Stevie Smith, quoted in the book *One Man and His Bike* by Mike Carter. Together with Jason Lewis in 1994, Smith embarked from London on Expedition 360, an attempt to circumnavigate the world without wind or motor assistance. The expedition makes Smith well-qualified to discuss the motivational effects of start and finish lines. Lewis became the first person to complete the feat in 2007, and Smith reached as far as Hawaii.

SEE ALSO
The Goal-Gradient Effect, *216*
Nine-Enders, *226*

THE MOST IMPORTANT
ROLE OF A
FINISHING LINE

is to

HERE
GOES

GET YOU
OVER THE
START LINE

TO SUCCEED
IN LIFE YOU NEED 3 THINGS:

a WISHBONE,

a BACKBONE

and a
FUNNY BONE.

— POPULARIZED BY REBA MCENTIRE

NOTES

Should you find yourself inspired to look deeper into any of the ideas explored by the sketches in this book, a great place to start would be the sources that inspired them.

PG. 8 / YOU GET WHAT YOU MEASURE

Quote from *The Art of Doing Science and Engineering* by Richard W. Hamming, pg. 202.

PG. 10 / THE SWISS CHEESE MODEL

"Revisiting the 'Swiss Cheese' Model Of Accidents" by J. Reason, E. Hollnagel and J Paries.

PG. 12 / SOLAR SYSTEM SIZES

I learned this from Dr. James O'Donoghue's superb YouTube channel, Interplanetary, where he explains many space facts.

PG. 16 / HOW TO WIN AT MONOPOLY

The Monopoly tips are drawn from gaming expert interviews in Joanna Fentozzi's *Business Insider* piece, "7 Monopoly hacks to ensure that you win every time."

PG. 22 / HITCHED TO THE UNIVERSE

The quote is from John Muir's book *My First Summer in the Sierra* and the lake featured is Heart Lake in California's Sierra Nevada mountains.

PG. 24 / SCHADENFREUDE

For a mini intro, try Tiffany Watt Smith's TED Ideas article "Do you secretly feel good when others stumble? 5 ways to make peace with this very human emotion."

PG. 26 / SURVIVORSHIP BIAS

Silent evidence—the evidence that we don't or can't readily choose to consider—is a term from Nassim Nicholas Taleb's *The Black Swan: The Impact of the Highly Improbable.*

PG. 36 / WHO CUT DOWN THE LAST TREE?

The quote is from Jared Diamond's article "Easter's End" in *Discover Magazine.*

PG. 38 / THE TRAVELING SALESMAN PROBLEM

The challenges and rewards of solving the traveling salesman problem are discussed by Marcus Wohlsen in "The Astronomical Math Behind UPS' New Tool to Deliver Packages Faster" in *Wired.*

PG. 50 / THE PARADOX OF CHOICE

Check out *The Paradox of Choice: Why More is Less* by Barry Schwartz and his TED Talk of the same name.

PG. 62 / THE THIRD TEACHER

The third teacher approach was pioneered by educator Loris Malaguzzi.

PG. 66 / MICROADVENTURE

See *Microadventures* by Alastair Humphreys and *alastairhumphreys.com/microadventures/.*

PG. 70 / HOPE

See *The Psychology of Hope* by C.R. Snyder. I first heard about it from Brené Brown's *Dare to Lead.*

PG. 74 / DAYS OF THE WEEK

As a wonderful introduction to the Norse myths and gods, you could do much worse than the entertaining and beautiful *Usborne Illustrated Norse Myths* (upon which the characters in the sketch are based), which our 9-year-old commanded me to read.

PG. 78 / THE OVERVIEW EFFECT

The sketch is based on the image of Earth from the moon taken on the Apollo 11 mission.

PG. 84 / ORDERING ADJECTIVES

Mark Forsyth's *The Elements of Eloquence: How to Turn the Perfect English Phrase* is an entertaining tour of writing techniques with fancy names, including this unconscious adjective rule.

PG. 86 / THE FINGER-DIP TEST

Certain plants, like cacti and orchids, live by different watering rules. I learned this from the good people at Patch Plants and their resident plant expert Alice Vincent (@noughticulture).

PG. 104 / NOTICE WHEN YOU'RE HAPPY

If This Isn't Nice, What Is?: Advice to the Young by Kurt Vonnegut.

PG. 108 / LAKE EFFECT SNOW

For everyday weather-related phenomena explained, see Dennis Mersereau's *The Skies Above*. He is also the source of the lovely phrase "nature's greatest snow machine."

PG. 114 / THE LAW OF UNINTENDED CONSEQUENCES

The simple formulation of unintended consequences arising whenever we try to regulate a complex system using a simple system is from economics professor Alex Tabarrok.

The workplace privacy example is known as the transparency paradox. The example about Bogotá traffic is from the Freakonomics Radio podcast episode on the cobra effect.

PG. 118 / MAZE VS. LABYRINTH

I based the sketches on the hedge maze at Henry VIII's Hampton Court Palace, near where we live, and the Lands End Labyrinth of San Francisco, near where we used to live.

The original from the Greek myth of Theseus and the Minotaur was complex and confusing, unlike the labyrinths that have evolved from it.

PG. 120 / HOW TO SPEAK PLAINLY

All the *Winnie-the-Pooh* books are lovely to read: *Winnie-the-Pooh, The House at Pooh Corner, When We Were Very Young* and *Now We Are Six*. The quote is from *The House at Pooh Corner*. Or, if you prefer to have the wisdom called out, try *The Tao of Pooh* by Benjamin Hoff.

PG. 122 / A WORLD OF FOUR INCOME LEVELS

For more, check out Hans Rosling's books *Factfulness* and *Gapminder*. And you could do much worse than watching his entertaining TED Talk "The best stats you've ever seen."

PG. 130 / 1.5 BILLION HEARTBEATS

This gem, and many other fascinating insights about size, scale, nature and physics, I learned from *Scale* by Geoffrey West.

PG. 132 / JOHARI WINDOW

The Johari window was designed by psychologists Joseph Luft and Harry Ingham (the name is a combination of their first names). The examples in the quadrants were shared with me by Nicola Rowledge.

PG. 134 / THE BS ASYMMETRY PRINCIPLE

Check out the book from the professors of the University of Washington iSchool class, Carl T. Bergstrom and Jevin D. West: *Calling Bullshit: The Art of Skepticism in a Data-Driven World*.

See also Williamson's "Take the time and effort to correct misinformation" in *Nature*.

PG. 136 / PROXEMICS

Proxemics was coined by the cultural anthropologist Edward T. Hall. Check out his book *The Hidden Dimension*. The cathedral and confession booth example is from professor, author and CEO of Jump Associates Dev Patnaik.

PG. 138 / DECIMAL VS. BINARY

For a readable visual introduction to the history and operation of computers—from binary, logic gates, transistors, circuits and Moore's law through software and AI—you could do a lot worse than my dad's book, *The Computing Universe* by Tony Hey and Gyuri Pápay.

PG. 140 / THE SQUARE-CUBE LAW

For this and other fascinating insights of scaling, check out the book *Scale* by Geoffrey West.

PG. 142 / AN IDLING CAR

The 150 balloons reference is from the GOV.UK article "Idling drivers could face higher fines under new government crackdown": *gov.uk/government/news/idling-drivers-could-face-higher-fines-under-new-government-crackdown*.

PG. 144 / THE TRUST EQUATION

Charles Green has written about the trust equation in several books, including *The Trusted Advisor*.

PG. 146 / POLLUTION IS HIGHLY LOCALIZED

I first read about this in a *BBC Science Focus* article, but see for example "'I am an air quality scientist' – Using citizen science to characterize school children's exposure to air pollution" by Diana Varaden, Einar Leidland Shanon Lim and Benjamin Barratt: *pubmed.ncbi.nlm.nih.gov/34166662/*.

PG. 154 / THE 10 ESSENTIALS FOR WILDERNESS SAFETY

The 10 essentials are drawn from the systems approach in *Mountaineering: The Freedom of the Hills* by the Mountaineers. They also have a day hiker's 10 essentials guide if you're planning something smaller.

PG. 160 / THE FOUR HORSEMEN OF RELATIONSHIP APOCALYPSE

The four horsemen and their antidotes are explained at *gottman.com/blog/the-four-horsemen-recognizing-criticism-contempt-defensiveness-and-stonewalling/*.

PG. 168 / THE IKEA EFFECT

Dan Ariely explains the IKEA effect in several videos online, or you can read the full paper: "The IKEA Effect: When Labor Leads to Love" by Michael Norton, Daniel Mochon and Dan Ariely: *hbs.edu/faculty/Pages/item.aspx?num=41121*.

PG. 172 / WEATHER VS. CLIMATE

"Why Is the Cold Weather So Extreme if the Earth Is Warming?" by Kendra Pierre-Louis in *The New York Times*.

PG. 178 / TECTONIC PLATE BOUNDARIES

Bill Bryson's *A Short History of Nearly Everything* covers the fascinating twists and turns of the plate tectonic theory's development and ultimate acceptance.

PG. 194 / HOW TO PEEL A STICKY NOTE

I learned this technique from the smart folks at Jump Associates, where we used a lot of Post-its. I believe they learned it from some people at Post-it manufacturer 3M.

PG. 210 / SPOTLIGHT EFFECT

"The Spotlight Effect in Social Judgment: An Egocentric Bias in Estimates of the Salience of One's Own Actions and Appearance" by Thomas Gilovich, Victoria Medvec and Kenneth Savitsky.

PG. 214 / THE POTATO RADIUS

The potato radius and other remarkable aspects of nature are shared on the show *Forces of Nature with Brian Cox*.

PG. 216 / GOAL-GRADIENT EFFECT

See "Why Feeling Close to the Finish Line Makes You Push Harder" by Katy Milkman and Kassie Brabaw in *Scientific American*.

PG. 224 / TRUST BATTERY

Tobi Lütke discusses the trust battery metaphor in a *New York Times* interview with Adam Bryant: "Tobi Lütke of Shopify: Powering a Team With a 'Trust Battery'."

PG. 226 / NINE-ENDERS

Daniel H. Pink discusses nine-enders and other quirks of timing in his book *When: The Scientific Secrets of Perfect Timing*. Also see "People search for meaning when they approach a new decade in chronological age" by Adam L. Alter and Hal E. Hershfield.

PG. 230 / THE THREE-DAY EFFECT

See Florence Williams's post on the REI blog: "The Nature Fix: The Three-Day Effect," *rei.com/blog/camp/the-nature-fix-the-three-day-effect*.

PG. 242 / YAK SHAVING

The yak drawing is in the style of Alison Green and Adam Stower's excellent children's book *What Can You Stack on the Back of a Yak?*.

PG. 244 / DON'T ASK THE BARBER IF YOU NEED A HAIRCUT

Warren Buffet famously shared the phrase, though it appears in several earlier forms.

PG. 250 / THE SHAPES OF STORIES

Kurt Vonnegut explains the story shapes in several entertaining videos online and discusses them in his books *A Man Without a Country* and *Palm Sunday*.

PG. 252 / HORIZONTAL VS. VERTICAL PUPILS

I based this sketch on the fascinating, informed discussion of the optics of animal pupils in "Why do animal eyes have pupils of different shapes?" by Martin S. Banks et al.

PG. 254 / SKIP ROCKS LIKE A PRO

Mark Rober's brilliant YouTube channel combines science and engineering with fun. These tips are from his video "Rock Skip Robot- The Science of Perfect Rock Skipping."

PG. 262 / THE BENJAMIN FRANKLIN EFFECT

David McRaney covers the psychology behind the effect in *You Are Not So Smart*. The story is shared by Ben Franklin himself in *The Autobiography of Benjamin Franklin*.

PG. 264 / SLEEP BASICS

Matt Walker, professor of neuroscience and psychology at the University of California, Berkeley, has written extensively about sleep (see *Why We Sleep: The New Science of Sleep and Dreams*) and features in many videos and podcasts, such as the Sleeping with Science TED series from which this content is drawn.

PG. 266 / WALKING SPEEDS

Geoffrey West discusses walking speeds on pgs. 335–336 of *Scale*.

PG. 270 / THE SUPPORTERS' PARADOX

The research on sports and happiness is by George McKerron and collaborators of the University of Sussex, England and conducted through the Mappiness app.

INDEX

ACKNOWLEDGMENTS

I'm always driven by sharing. The joy of ideas is that they share so well compared to physical things. So I'm thrilled to have the opportunity to share these ideas and this project with more people through this book. I have everyone at Media Lab to thank for that, in particular: Tim Baker, Jeff Ashworth, Glen Karpowich, Tara Sherman, Madeline Raynor, Dave Weiss, Susan Dazzo, Noreen Henson and especially Phil Sexton for believing in my potential.

So many people have given me emotional and financial support over the years. Thanks so much to my patrons for supporting me directly, in some cases for years—I wouldn't have managed this without you. Thanks to the kind souls who've voluntarily bought me coffee to help me keep working on my sketches. Thanks to those who've sent me supportive notes along the way and those who've downloaded sketches to use and share in their presentations, at work or with their networks. Thanks to everyone who's shared sketch ideas with me. Thanks to those who've pointed out where I've made mistakes or when I needed to up my game. And a massive thanks to my close friends and family, especially my brother, Chris, for the constant encouragement and for being such great cheerleaders and sounding boards for me.

I'm standing on others' shoulders through the ideas I'm sharing. Thanks to all whose ideas and work feature in this book and have influenced my life. I've referenced your work in the Notes and pointed people to where they can learn more. Please get in touch if something needs correcting.

As with so many things, when I get a sketch right, it can make the concept look simple. But in reality, I've spent a lot of time working on sketches over the last 10 years. For that, I need to thank our two boys—this project has coincided almost completely with their lives—and especially my wife, Maria. Her love, patience, support, honest feedback and putting up with me disappearing on evenings, weekends and even Friday nights for years as I followed this unusual mission has been astonishing. Thank you.

JONO HEY is the creator of *Sketchplanations*, where he's been explaining the world one sketch at a time for more than a decade. He's lived in Europe and the U.S., working across academia, business, design, product development, entrepreneurship, strategy and engineering and helping create two successful companies. He holds a Ph.D. from the University of California at Berkeley and a master's degree in engineering from the University of Bath. You'll also find his unique illustrations in Bill Gates's 2022 book *How to Prevent the Next Pandemic*. He does his sketching from London where he lives with his wife and two boys. Find the latest at *sketchplanations.com*.

Media Lab Books
For inquiries, contact customerservice@topixmedia.com

Copyright 2024 Jono Hey

Published by Topix Media Lab
14 Wall Street, Suite 3C
New York, NY 10005

Printed in China

ISBN-13: 978-1-956403-57-2
ISBN-10: 1-956403-57-4

CEO Tony Romando

Vice President & Publisher Phil Sexton
Senior Vice President of Sales & New Markets Tom Mifsud
Vice President of Retail Sales & Logistics Linda Greenblatt
Chief Financial Officer Vandana Patel
Vice President of Manufacturing & Distribution Nancy Puskuldjian
Digital Marketing & Strategy Manager Elyse Gregov

Chief Content Officer Jeff Ashworth
Senior Acquisitions Editor Noreen Henson
Creative Director Susan Dazzo
Photo Director Dave Weiss
Managing Editor Tara Sherman

Project Editor Tim Baker
Project Designer Glen Karpowich
Features Editor Trevor Courneen
Associate Editor Juliana Sharaf
Designers Alyssa Bredin Quirós, Mikio Sakai
Copy Editor & Fact Checker Madeline Raynor
Assistant Photo Editor Jenna Addesso
Assistant Managing Editor Claudia Acevedo